A GUIDE TO
CO-TEACHING
WITH PARAEDUCATORS

*We proudly dedicate this book
to the paraeducators we know and
have worked with as well as all the other
paraeducators who make possible the physical,
academic, and social inclusion of diverse students
in mixed-ability classrooms. Thank you for
facilitating a sense of belonging, mastery,
independence, and generosity for
our children and youth.*

A GUIDE TO
CO-TEACHING
WITH PARAEDUCATORS

Practical Tips for K–12 Educators

ANN I. NEVIN

RICHARD A. VILLA

JACQUELINE S. THOUSAND

A Joint Publication

CORWIN PRESS
A SAGE Company

Council for
Exceptional
Children

For information:

Corwin Press
A SAGE Company
2455 Teller Road
Thousand Oaks, California 91320
www.corwinpress.com

SAGE Ltd.
1 Oliver's Yard
55 City Road
London, EC1Y 1SP
United Kingdom

SAGE India Pvt. Ltd.
B 1/I 1 Mohan Cooperative
    Industrial Area
Mathura Road, New Delhi 110 044
India

SAGE Asia-Pacific Pte. Ltd.
33 Pekin Street #02-01
Far East Square
Singapore 048763

Printed in the United States of America.

Library of Congress Cataloging-in-Publication Data

Nevin, Ann.
A guide to co-teaching with paraeducators : practical tips for K–12 educators / by Ann I. Nevin, Richard A. Villa, and Jacqueline S. Thousand.
     p. cm.
Includes bibliographical references and index.
ISBN 978-1-4129-5763-2 (cloth) — ISBN 978-1-4129-5764-9 (pbk.)
1. Teaching teams. 2. Inclusive education. I. Villa, Richard A., 1952-
II. Thousand, Jacqueline S., 1950-
III. Title.

LB1029.T4N48 2009
371.9'046—dc22

2008020173
This book is printed on acid-free paper.

12 10 9 8 7 6 5 4 3 2

Acquisitions Editor: David Chao
Editorial Assistant: Mary Dang
Production Editor: Appingo Publishing Services
Cover Designer: Michael Dubowe

Contents

Acknowledgments

Corwin Press gratefully acknowledges the contributions of the following individuals:

Jodie Beecher
Graphic Designer
Pace University
New York, NY

Mari Gates
Educator
Henry B. Burkland Intermediate School
Middleboro, MA

Charlotte Kenney
8th-Grade Math and Science Teacher
Browns River Middle School
Jericho, VT

Robert Kuchta
Biology and Chemistry Teacher; Curriculum Assistant
Chippewa Falls Senior High School
Chippewa Falls, WI

Melissa Miller
Science Educator
Lynch Middle School
Farmington, AR

About the Authors

Jacqueline Thousand, Richard Villa, and Ann Nevin

Ann I. Nevin, PhD, is Professor Emerita, Arizona State University, and Visiting Professor, Florida International University. Author of books, research articles, and numerous chapters, Ann is recognized for her scholarship and dedication to providing meaningful, practice-oriented, research-based strategies for teachers to integrate students with special learning needs. Since the 1970s, she has co-developed various innovative teacher education programs that affect many kinds of personnel, including paraeducators. Programs include the Vermont Consulting Teacher Program, Collaborative Consultation Project Re-Tool sponsored by the Council for Exceptional Children, the Arizona State University program for special educators to infuse self-determination skills throughout the curriculum, and the Urban SEALS (Special Education Academic Leaders) doctoral program at Florida International University. Her advocacy, research, and teaching spans more than 38 years of working with a diverse array of people to help students with disabilities succeed in normalized school environments. In recognition of her lifetime achievements, Dr. Nevin received the 2007 Landis M. Stetler Award from the Florida Council for Exceptional Children, for individuals who have made a significant contribution to the education of children and youths with exceptionalities. Dr. Nevin is known for action-oriented presentations, workshops, and classes that are designed to meet the individual needs of participants by encouraging introspection and personal discovery for optimal learning.

Richard A. Villa, EdD, has worked with thousands of teachers and administrators throughout North America. In addition, Dr. Villa has provided technical assistance to the departments of education of the United States, Canada, Vietnam, Scotland, Laos, Britain, and Honduras. His primary field of expertise is the development of administrative and instructional support systems for educating all students within general education settings. Dr. Villa has been a middle and high school classroom teacher, special educator, special education coordinator, pupil personal services director, and director of instructional services. He has authored over 100 articles and book chapters regarding inclusive education, differentiated instruction, collaborative planning, teaching, co-teaching, and school restructuring. Displaying an enthusiastic, knowledgeable, and humorous style of teaching, Dr. Villa is a gifted communicator who has the conceptual, technical, and interpersonal skills to facilitate change in education. His professional development activities have included short-term keynote addresses and papers presented at national and international conferences, two-day guided practice workshops for school teams, three- to five-day programs, three-week intensive workshops, and semester-long (15-week) programs offered through universities.

Jacqueline S. Thousand, PhD, is a professor in the College of Education at California State University San Marcos, where she directs special education professional preparation and master's programs. Prior to coming to California, she directed Inclusion Facilitator and Early Childhood Special Education graduate and postgraduate professional preparation programs at the University of Vermont. She also coordinated several federal grants, all concerned with providing professional development for educators to facilitate the inclusion of students with disabilities in local schools. Known for her creative, fun-filled, action-oriented teaching style, Dr. Thousand is a nationally recognized teacher, author, systems change consultant, and advocate for disability rights and inclusive education. A versatile communicator, she has written numerous books, research articles, and chapters on issues related to inclusive schooling, organizational change, differentiated instruction and universal design, cooperative group learning, creative problem solving, and co-teaching and collaborative planning with multiple partners, including paraeducators. She is actively involved in international teacher education endeavors and serves on the editorial boards of several national and international journals.

Introduction

Our (the authors') purpose in writing this book was to showcase the role of paraeducators who work in inclusive education settings, in particular those who work with co-teachers. As we delved into what experts and researchers had discovered, we learned about the multitude of titles that have typically been applied to paraeducators: aides, paraprofessionals, educational assistants, teaching assistants, TAs, individual aides, personal aides, individual assistants, paras, and paraeducators. All of these titles refer to a person who is not a certificated professional but who has responsibilities to a child or group of children in a school setting.

Each of the authors has had unique experiences with paraeducators as part of his or her own development. For example, for two years Ann Nevin served as a tutor for emergent readers in a third-grade inclusive classroom in Florida and as a teacher's aide to master teachers in speed reading and the writer's process during 10 consecutive summers at a 10-day camp for teenagers in California. Rich Villa can vividly remember being a new science teacher for grades 7–12 and not knowing how best to work with the paraeducator assigned to him. Subsequently as a special educator, Rich worked with several paraeducators and found that they were critical and valuable colleagues assisting in the delivery of instruction to support students with Individual Education Programs (IEPs). In addition, when he later served as a district administrator, he actively recruited, trained, and arranged for a paraeducator to serve as an elected member of a staff development committee and arranged for paraeducators to receive training and attend IEP meetings. Jacqueline Thousand's experiences include working with paraeducators in community early education programs for young children with disabilities and teaching paraeducators who were enrolled in teacher certification programs. These experiences form the basis of our deep respect for the role that paraeducators play in the lives of students and teachers.

As the book unfolds, you—the reader—will learn how the presence of paraeducators in the classroom helps to ensure that individual students can receive differentiated instruction to meet their diverse needs. The content of each chapter focuses on effective instructional practices and includes problem–solution scenarios based on real-life experiences of paraeducators in inclusive classrooms and the educators with whom they work.

We wrote this book to be as user-friendly as possible. At the beginning of each chapter is some visual representation of its contents as a preview, to prepare you for what you will learn. We used a variety of visual representations such as concept maps, timelines, and organizational charts. We posed questions to stimulate your curiosity—the questions reflect comprehension, evaluation, and application levels of understanding. In addition, we sprinkled charts, forms, lesson plans, and other reproducible items throughout the book so as to facilitate the day-to-day work of the co-teacher teams and their paraeducators. We liberally used text scaffolding techniques that help readers remember and track content (e.g., flowcharts, charts to show comparisons and contrasts, graphic organizers, and note-taking guides).

We wanted to let the paraeducators' "voice" and experience come through. And we wanted to write in such a way that *all* who care about the work of the paraeducator can find the book useful in guiding their work with paraeducators. That's why we hope that parents, teachers, school board members, and related service personnel such as speech therapists and guidance counselors will use this book. Our goal is to help all our readers add new reasons to respect and advance the work of paraeducators in our schools.

1

Why Paraeducators?

What Experience, History, Law, and Research Say!

Figure 1.1
Paraeducators in Schools: A Time Line of Key Historical Events

1950s	1970s	1990s	2000s
↓	↓	↓	↓
Traditional clerical roles	Transformed to instructional roles	Increased classroom roles by 65% Research on paraeducators' roles begins to appear in the literature.	Increased role of paraeducators working in inclusive classrooms to support students with disabilities; others are assigned to work with students in specialized classrooms (e.g., Title I, English language learning programs), computer labs, and libraries Research on paraeducators' impact begins to appear in the literature.
	● **1975** The Education for All Handicapped Children Act (P. L. 94-142) adds responsibilities for students with disabilities.	● **1997** The Individuals with Disabilities Education Act is amended to requires students with disabilities to have access to general education curriculum and instruction; thus many paraeducators accompany their students into general education classrooms.	● **2001** The No Child Left Behind Act (NCLB) adds responsibility for teachers to supervise paraeducators and district responsibility to ensure professional development for highly qualified personnel and minimum standards for employment. ● **2004** The Individuals with Disabilities Education Improvement Act (IDEIA) adds requirement for paraeducators to participate in professional development activities.

The time line in Figure 1.1 shows that there are many key historical events that have influenced the way paraeducators work in today's classrooms. As we begin, you may already be wondering:

- What are paraeducators?
- When did paraeducators first become a part of the American classroom?
- What does the research say about paraeducators?
- What are the current legislative mandates regarding paraeducators?
- What are the potential legal challenges?

In this chapter, you will learn the answers to these questions as they relate to paraeducators who work in inclusive classrooms.

■ WHAT PARAEDUCATORS ARE

First, what do we mean by the terms *paraeducator, inclusive education*, and *co-teaching*? In addition to being defined below, these and other terms that may be unfamiliar are found in the Glossary.

A *paraeducator* is a school employee who "provides instructional, safety, and/or therapeutic services to students" (French, 2008a, p. 1). Paraeducators work under the supervision of a professional in a position that might have one of the following titles: teaching assistant, paraprofessional, aide, instructional aide, health care aide, educational technician, literacy or math tutor, job coach, instructional assistant, or educational assistant. The two most frequently used terms for describing a person in this role are *paraprofessional* and *paraeducator*. For example, the term *paraprofessional* is used in the U.S. federal law that governs the education of students with disabilities (IDEIA, 2004, Part D, Section 651). The term *paraeducator* has been used by some leading authors in the field, such as Pickett and Gerlach (2003), who speak from the perspective of paraeducators themselves. To honor the perspective of and to reflect the increased instructional role of paraprofessionals, in this book we use the term *paraeducator*.

Inclusive education, in our (the authors') view, is a process where schools welcome, value, support, and empower all students in shared environments and experiences for the purpose of attaining the goals of education. *Co-teaching* is two or more people sharing responsibility for teaching some or all of the students assigned to a classroom (Villa, Thousand, & Nevin, 2008a). Co-teaching involves distributing responsibility among people for planning, instructing, and evaluating the performance of students in a classroom. Co-teaching is one example of an inclusive educational practice that allows general education teachers and others to provide students with and without disabilities access to the general education curriculum.

■ THE INTRODUCTION OF PARAEDUCATORS TO THE AMERICAN CLASSROOM

The history of paraeducators began in the 1950s, when they were introduced into schools to provide teachers more time for planning for instruction. For the most part, early paraeducators performed clerical services. They duplicated materials and they managed students in non-instructional settings such as the lunchroom or playground.

In the 1970s, federal legislation was passed that guaranteed students with disabilities access to a free appropriate public education. With the steady movement toward general education being the preferred primary placement for students with disabilities, the paraeducator's role has evolved and is now primarily instructional in nature, especially when supporting students in the general education setting (Giangreco, Smith, & Pinckney, 2006; Pickett, 2002).

The increased reliance on paraeducators to assist in differentiating instruction in the classroom is evidenced by the numbers. For example, a comprehensive study of K–12 staffing patterns in all 50 states (National Center for Education Statistics, 2000) revealed that in the seven-year period from 1993 to 2000, the number of paraeducators in classrooms increased from approximately 319,000 to over 525,000, a 65% increase. Over half a million paraeducators were employed in inclusive and other educational settings supporting students with disabilities—the rest were assigned to support students in compensatory programs (e.g., Title I aides or multilingual aides). Some paraeducators worked in learning environments such as libraries, media centers, and computer laboratories. These data reveal the predominantly instructional nature of today's paraeducators.

MEET PARAEDUCATORS: ■
MS. O. AND MS. BEGAY

The many and varied roles of paraeducators also have been reported in the literature. Paraeducators usually discover they wear multiple hats as they juggle their roles and responsibilities. For example, paraeducators can be note-takers for students with hearing impairments as they attend classes (Yarger, 1996) or translators as well as tutors for children who speak languages other than English (Wenger et al., 2004). Teaching pro-social behaviors to young children (Perez & Murdock, 1999) and serving as aides to coach appropriate behavior for students with autism have been shown to be effective (Young, 1997). Paraeducators have also served as speech-language assistants (Radaszewski-Byrne, 1997), job coaches (Rogan & Held, 1999), or tutors for helping students learn to read, compute, or write (Ashbaker & Morgan, 2000). Other, more subtle, roles have included paraeducators as cultural ambassadors who help educational personnel bridge the gap between monolingual professionals and bilingual communities (Koroloff, 1996; Rueda & Monzo, 2002) and those who help all the children in addition to those specifically assigned to them (Giangreco et al., 2006; Marks, Schrader, & Levine, 1999). Moreover, paraeducators are active in college classrooms to provide accommodations (Burgstahler, Duclos, & Turcotte, 1999).

Pamela O. serves as an example of a paraeducator who juggled multiple roles as part of her job in an inclusive multicultural magnet school for the arts in Miami, Florida. She instructed tutorials, provided playground supervision, and prepared materials. She worked for two years with a team of co-teachers who practiced "looping," where they followed their third-graders when they were promoted to fourth grade (see Nevin, Cramer, Salazar, & Voigt, 2007). Ms. O. knew the fourth-grade curriculum because previously she had been a paraeducator for the fourth grade. She had some unique gifts that helped her relate to her students, such as her creativity in helping them construct posters to visually represent what they were learning. In fact, her general education teacher complimented her communication skills: "She's not bilingual but she understands Spanish (her husband speaks Spanish) and she can speak basics to the kids. For example, the Cuban kids will go up to her and ask for help with no problem" (R. Puga, personal communication, May 24, 2006). Ms. O. was especially grateful for the added skills she learned when the guidance counselor included her in once-a-week social skills discussions and activities for the fourth-graders to learn to tolerate and respect each others' differences. In her role as playground aide, she often asked the students to use those skills when they were involved in arguments at recess.

Another example of a paraeducator who juggled multiple roles at a junior high school is reported in a study conducted by Nevin, Malian, et al. (2007). Ms. Begay spoke English and Dakota Sioux and had worked for several years in other roles prior to becoming a paraeducator. She explained her work in a junior high school this way: "I work [in a classroom] with sixth-graders [where I tutor] in math and science, seventh-graders in science and social studies, where there are 10 students with disabilities. The students are learning to speak English as a second language, as they are all Native Americans. [Many of my students have] behavior issues due to lack of academic self-esteem." Ms. Begay reported that she helped her students work in cooperative learning groups and as peer tutors. She firmly believed that the student who has trouble learning represents an instructional challenge rather than a "problem student." She reported that she received support for how to differentiate her instruction and that her classroom routines helped meet the needs of her learners. She said that to prepare for her lessons, she reviewed lesson plans with her co-teacher. She emphasized to the authors of the study that the most important part of her job in the inclusive classroom was "to assist my students with strategies that are easier to understand. I make my special education students feel good about learning."

◼ WHAT THE RESEARCH SAYS ABOUT PARAEDUCATORS

In Chapter 3, you will discover more about the roles and responsibilities of paraeducators. Regardless of role, the literature is clear about the value of paraeducators in the classroom. For example, students with disabilities are included more in classroom activities when paraeducators are present. The presence of paraeducators makes it possible for *all* students' instruction to be differentiated. General educators appreciate the presence of paraeducators, who are considered essential for supporting students eligible for special education in their classrooms (Downing, Ryndak, & Clark, 2000;

Giangreco, Broer, & Edelman, 2002; Marks et al., 1999; Mueller & Murphy, 2001; Piletic, Davis, & Aschemeier, 2005; Riggs & Mueller, 2001; Villa et al., 2008a).

The California Department of Education has recognized 22 California sites for their collaborative approaches to including all students in inclusive environments. In such collaborative cultures, paraeducators often are given the same inservice training, are sent to conferences and workshops, and are asked to share their experiences with professional colleagues. Paraeducators also experience the benefits of being appreciated. For example, at Rincon Middle School in Escondido, California, the special education department chair said that people wanted to "transfer to Rincon because of the way instructional assistants are treated here. They are a part of the team: valued, respected, given the ability to make decisions" (Grady, 2007, p. 7).

Paraeducators from underrepresented populations (particularly those from marginalized populations, such as those who are culturally and linguistically diverse) can offer new perspectives and support for both children and teachers. As Ashbaker and Morgan (2000) suggest, paraeducators who are themselves bilingual can serve as role models as well as ambassadors who help teachers better understand the impact of culture and language on learning outcomes.

Parents and family members also appreciate what paraeducators do. They are clear about their preferences for how paraeducators might work with their children (French & Chopra, 1999; Palmer, Borthwick-Duffy, Widaman, & Best, 1998). For example, French and Chopra (1999) report the results of an exploratory focus group process involving mothers of 23 children who received special education services in general education classrooms, mainly through support from paraeducators. The paraeducators were believed to be compassionate and dedicated people who were important to the parents. Especially valued were their roles as team members, instructors, caregivers, and health needs providers.

Although parents are clear that paraeducators can be beneficial in their children's education (French & Chopra, 1999), they are cautious and remain apprehensive about the quality of education their child actually receives in inclusive classrooms (Palmer et al., 1998). The most frequently identified problem is that the paraeducators often have limited training and support, which results in high levels of staff turnover. Parents want paraeducators and classroom teachers who work with their children to receive appropriate training and supervision. In addition, parents appreciate paraeducators who are creative about facilitating peer relationships. Paraeducators can do a lot to make sure that students assigned to them are not isolated and further stigmatized. Parents insist that the following issues should be handled before their child works with any paraeducator (Paula Goldberg[1], Executive Director of the PACER Center):

---

1. For more information, visit the Council for Exceptional Children's Web page "Improving Paraeducator Practices." The home page is at http://www.cec.sped.org. Click on "Professional Practice Topics and Info," then "Paraeducators."

- Be sure paraeducators know the child's disability, techniques for positive behavior support, how to communicate with the child, and approaches to encourage independence and peer relationships.
- Paraeducators need clearly defined roles and responsibilities, which should ideally be written into the child's academic, behavior, or language development plan.
- Parents want paraeducators to be included in their child's team meetings and want them to update them on their child's progress.

What do children say about working with paraeducators? Children's voices are strikingly absent from the literature. Recently, some researchers have studied how children and youths talk about their paraeducators (e.g., Giangreco, Yuan, McKenzie, Cameron, & Flalka, 2005; Skär & Tam, 2001; Werts, Zigmond, & Leeper, 2001). Thirteen children and adolescents (aged from 8 to 19 years) with restricted mobility who lived in northern Sweden were interviewed (Skär & Tam, 2001). The results of the interviews yielded five distinctions with respect to their perceptions of their assistants. Some perceived their assistant as a substitute for their parent (mother or father). Others perceived their assistant as a professional or as a friend. All students could articulate how the "ideal assistant" should work with them. In other words, children from age 8 to 19 have formed very distinct perceptions of their relationships with their paraeducators. Some interactions were perceived as unequal and ambivalent. The results of this study emphasize the importance of clearly defining and clarifying the roles of paraeducators not only for paraeducators themselves, but for the educators who work with and supervise them as well as the students they serve. A paraeducator is not meant to be a substitute parent or friend; instead, he or she is meant to be an educational support person. With that said, because paraeducators often are quite sensitive to their students' views and interests, it is important for them to be able to share their perceptions.

■ CURRENT LEGISLATIVE MANDATES REGARDING PARAEDUCATORS

What do current legislative mandates suggest? Changes in paraeducators' multiple roles that have been reported by researchers are now officially part of recent legislation. The No Child Left Behind Act (NCLB, 2001) and the Individuals with Disabilities Education Improvement Act (IDEIA, 2004) have articulated several requirements for paraeducators. NCLB sets out the minimum requirements. Namely, paraeducators must complete at least two years of postsecondary study, obtain an associate's degree from a community college, or demonstrate knowledge of and ability to assist in instructing in reading, writing, and mathematics by passing a formal state or local academic assessment. Many paraeducators who were hired prior to the enactment of this legislation have had to participate in professional development activities in order to meet these requirements.

In contrast, IDEIA sets forth the specific guidelines for the content of professional development activities (Part D, Subpart 1, Section 651, 654). School systems and state departments of education must design comprehensive programs to empower paraeducators to learn how to teach and meet the needs of children with different learning styles and children who speak other languages than English. They also must learn to implement positive behavioral interventions and scientifically based reading and early literacy instruction. Other training must include helping paraeducators work with parents and families, teaching children with low incidence disabilities, and helping health professionals meet the needs of students with health, mobility, or behavior needs. Paraeducators must learn how to participate in collaborative meetings with others.

POTENTIAL LEGAL CHALLENGES ■

What are potential legal challenges for paraeducators who work in inclusive classrooms? Etscheidt (2005), in a comprehensive legal analysis of paraeducator services for students with disabilities, reminds us that "paraprofessionals may not serve as the sole designer, deliverer, or evaluator of a student's program" (p. 68). Stated another way, it is the teacher who has the responsibility for the education of all learners, even when instructional and other tasks are delegated or mutually decided upon by a teaching team.

Paraeducators are school employees who teach under the supervision of other professional staff responsible for the design, modification, implementation, and assessment of instruction and learner progress. Thus, Pickett and Gerlach (2003), national leaders in the training and supervision of paraeducators, emphasize the supervision of paraeducators. Yet, ambiguity as to who is responsible for the supervision of paraeducators and how supervision should be accomplished remains a premier problem. Clearly, co-teaching among educators and paraeducators creates a unique opportunity for the regular and authentic ongoing observation, analysis, and coaching of paraeducator effectiveness recommended by Ashbaker and Morgan (2001).

SUMMARY ■

To what extent do you feel that you have enough information to generate your own answers to the questions at the beginning of this chapter? For example, how would you answer the question "What is a paraeducator?" We hope you appreciate that your school district or state might use a title other than "paraeducator." We hope you also understand the history of how paraeducators have become a vital piece of the fabric that makes public school classrooms more successful for students.

Now that you know more about what researchers say about paraeducators, you may have even more questions. This may lead you to read the studies or even, in some cases, to conduct your own study. We hope your curiosity has been stimulated by the demands that current legislative mandates place on school administrators and teachers as well as paraeducators. In addition, we hope you can join forces with school personnel to help address the legal challenges that continue to arise.

The next chapter brings to life the varied roles, responsibilities, and challenges faced by paraeducators in real schools today. You will meet elementary, middle level, and secondary paraeducators and their co-teaching teams.

2

Meet the Teams

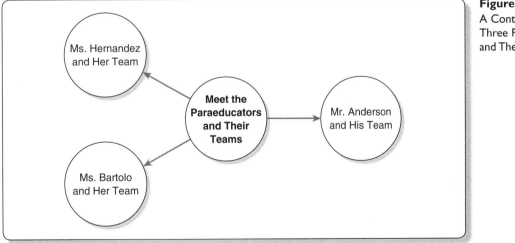

Figure 2.1
A Content Map of Three Paraeducators and Their Teams

I n this chapter, you will meet three paraeducators and their teaching teams, who will deal with several contemporary problems or issues that face paraeducators who work in inclusive classrooms. As you read about the three paraeducators, and as you learn a little bit about the members of their teams, ask yourself the following questions:

- What challenges will the paraeducators face when they begin to work with the members of their teams?

- How are their work situations similar or different compared to your own work situation or the situations of the paraeducators who work in your school?
- If you were the paraeducator for each of the three teams described in this chapter, what aspects of your situation would you perceive as positive or supportive?
- If you were the paraeducator for any of the three teams, what questions or concerns would you want to discuss with your supervisor or team members?

■ MEET MS. HERNANDEZ: THE ELEMENTARY SCHOOL PARAEDUCATOR AND HER TEAM

Ms. Hernandez has been working as a part-time special education paraeducator for the past year. She and her family live within walking distance of the Chaparral Valley Elementary School (CVES), which her two young children attend. They have lived in this community for seven years. CVES is the only school in the district that receives Title I funding to support math and literacy development and the only school in which a majority of the students receive standards-based English language development instruction during and after school. Ms. Hernandez's first language, and her husband's first language, is Spanish; both of their children speak Spanish as their primary language and have been enrolled in the voluntary dual immersion program.

In this classroom, English- and Spanish-speaking students are integrated in classrooms where they learn in Spanish for the majority of the day in the lower grades and increase the amount of English annually until they are learning in both languages for equal amounts of time. The goal of this program is to produce learners who have high proficiency in both languages and who can meet state and district academic standards.

Ms. Hernandez was recruited for the part-time special education paraeducator position because she had been so involved in her children's classrooms and because of her ability to communicate in both Spanish and English. She took the job originally to supplement her family's income so they could move to a larger apartment and also so she could be more directly involved on her children's school campus.

Dual immersion language programs are also known as two-way immersion education. For more information, see http://www.ed.govpubsToolsforSchools/2way.html.]

Last year, as a special education paraeducator, she was assigned to work with small groups of students eligible for special education in all of the grades except kindergarten. She primarily worked in a small resource room where another group might also be taught by the one full-time special educator and one part-time special educator who had just begun at this school.

Although Ms. Hernandez enjoyed learning about how to teach various reading and math programs in that setting, she also experienced a great deal of frustration with students who had difficulty attending to task.

Among the students with whom she worked were several boys who had difficulties getting along with one another. They all had Behavior Support Plans or Behavior Intervention Plans (BIPs; specially designed plans to improve their social interactions in the classroom) and spent much of their day together in the resource room rather than their respective general education classrooms. Ms. Hernandez knew that the full-time special education teacher, who supervised her, was co-teaching in general education classrooms for part of the day, as the principal had initiated the delivery of special education support in general education through co-teaching between the special educator and select classroom teachers. She wished she had the chance to get out of the resource room other than during lunch and recess times and be in general education classrooms.

This year began very differently for Ms. Hernandez and the entire school staff. Ms. Hernandez's principal, Suzanne Schmidt, a strong and proactive instructional leader, had stated on many occasions that she was on a path of crafting school-wide collaborative endeavors to increase the achievement of all students. To that end, during the previous spring semester and over the summer, the principal convened a group that included the reading specialist, the full-time special educator, teacher representatives from each grade level, and a university professor who had helped the faculty members develop their co-teaching skills. The group's charge was to rethink how reading and special education services could be integrated into a single team effort that would blend the expertise of all of the specialists in the building. A major concern of everyone on the team was that the restructuring of services might create a new type of homogenous tracking, where students with similar needs spend a large portion of their day with the same group of similarly performing students. The team agreed that they would put this on the weekly meeting agenda, so that students would not be taught in a new form of segregated instruction. As part of this effort, the team attended a local three-day institute on inclusion and Response to Intervention (RtI). Paraeducators were invited to attend, and with strong encouragement from the principal, Ms. Hernandez decided to go.

She was glad she did! She learned how the federal Individual with Disabilities Education Improvement Act of 2004 (IDEIA) emphasized early identification and prevention of children's learning difficulties though a three-tiered RtI approach.

At Tier 1, classroom teachers use research-based instructional strategies and interventions to improve core classroom instruction for all students. At Tier 2, students who have difficulties succeeding with Tier 1 instruction are provided with *supplemental* instruction in small groups, with data being collected on their progress on a regular basis. For students whose data suggest they are not responding to Tier 1 and Tier 2 supplemental instruction, Tier 3 intensified instruction is provided. Tier 3 intensified instruction may mean an increase in the length and frequency of interventions, a decrease in group size, a change in the intervention approach, and, in some cases, more formal evaluations in order to determine whether special education services may be needed. To Ms. Hernandez, all

See www.nrcld.org and Batsche, 2006, for more information on the three-tiered RtI approach.

Figure 2.2 Response to Intervention Academic and Behavioral Intervention Tiers

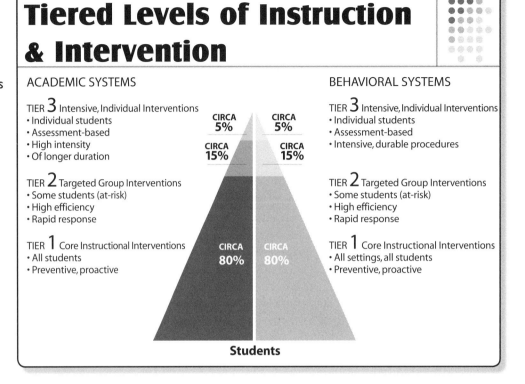

Tiered Levels of Instruction & Intervention

ACADEMIC SYSTEMS

TIER 3 Intensive, Individual Interventions
- Individual students
- Assessment-based
- High intensity
- Of longer duration

TIER 2 Targeted Group Interventions
- Some students (at-risk)
- High efficiency
- Rapid response

TIER 1 Core Instructional Interventions
- All students
- Preventive, proactive

BEHAVIORAL SYSTEMS

TIER 3 Intensive, Individual Interventions
- Individual students
- Assessment-based
- Intensive, durable procedures

TIER 2 Targeted Group Interventions
- Some students (at-risk)
- High efficiency
- Rapid response

TIER 1 Core Instructional Interventions
- All settings, all students
- Preventive, proactive

CIRCA 5%   CIRCA 5%
CIRCA 15%   CIRCA 15%
CIRCA 80%   CIRCA 80%

Students

of this made great sense, and she was pleased that the plan to redesign how people were going to work together this year was based upon what the team learned. She believed that it was very important that the three tiers would apply to reading and behavior. She found it helpful to refer to the graphic in Figure 2.2 because the visual representation of the three RtI tiers for academics and behavior helped her understand how everything fit together.

For Ms. Hernandez, the number of hours on the job increased. The principal had creatively budgeted some of the money to hire part-time literacy paraeducators at each grade level, which supplemented the special education dollars that funded Ms. Hernandez's position. This meant she now works five hours rather than three hours a day, from 8:15 a.m. until 1:15 p.m. Her responsibilities changed, too. Now she works with various groups of students with and without disabilities throughout the day in the second- and third-grade classrooms to which she is assigned. She was told that she was being assigned to those grades because most of the students had "below proficient" scores on district reading and math tests. Plus, her ability to communicate in both English and Spanish would be a great benefit at these grade levels, as there were still many students who were acquiring English language proficiency.

For Ms. Hernandez's second- and third-grade teams, there are three classroom teachers who teach 20 to 25 students, for a total of 70 to 75 students at each grade level. At each grade level, during a new differentiated literacy group time, students are regrouped across classes to form six

Name	Role	Responsibilities
Ms. Carlotta Hernandez	5-hour-per-day special education paraeducator	Provides instruction to small groups of students during *BRITE time* and supports classroom teachers during *homeroom* literacy or math instruction
Ms. Suzanne Schmidt	Principal of Chaparral Valley Elementary School	Ensures that *BRITE time* schedules and personnel are delivering instruction and meeting during weekly planning hour
Ms. Robin Dahl	Second-grade general education teacher	Delivers curriculum and during *BRITE time* provides differentiated instruction to the 20–25 second-grade students with the least need for support in reading instruction
Mr. Tim Drumming	Second-grade general education teacher	Delivers curriculum and provides literacy intervention to 20–25 *proficient* second-graders during *BRITE time*
Ms. Suyapa Prada	Dual immersion second-grade general education teacher	Delivers curriculum and provides literacy intervention to 6–10 "below proficient" second-graders
Ms. Wanda Waldrich	Reading specialist	Collaboratively works with the special educators and the principal to orchestrate *BRITE time* interventions for grades 2 through 5; manages the first-grade Reading Recovery program, literacy tutors; instructs small literacy groups during *BRITE time* for grades 2 through 5
Ms. Sidia Sooze	Speech, language, and hearing specialist	Provides speech, language, early literacy development direct instruction for students and consultative instruction to general and special education personnel
Ms. Melony Helprin	Full-time special education teacher	Manages the IEPs for second-, third-, fourth-, and fifth-graders eligible for special education; co-teaches in second- through fourth-grade general education classrooms, and instructs small literacy groups during *BRITE time* for grades 2 through 4

Table 2.1
Members of Ms. Hernandez's Second-Grade Team

different groupings of students. The school agreed to name this differentiated instruction time Block Reading Intervention Toward Excellence, or BRITE time. Each grade-level team meets on Wednesdays to examine data on students' literacy progress, form new groups of students based upon the data, and plan instruction for the next week.

Second-Grade Team

As shown in Table 2.1, Ms. Hernandez's second-grade team includes the three second-grade teachers—Ms. Robin Dahl, Mr. Tim Drumming, and Ms. Suyapa Prada—as well as the full-time special educator, Melony

Helprin, and the literacy specialist, Wanda Waldrich. The school's speech and language specialist, Sidia Sooze, also is on this team, because the principal and teachers are very aware of her specialized knowledge and expertise with regard to phonemic awareness, vocabulary development, and decoding.

In Ms. Hernandez's experience, the second-grade-level team is congenial and supportive of one another. As Ms. Hernandez's oldest daughter was in Ms. Prada's second-grade class last year, Ms. Hernandez knows Ms. Prada very well. Ms. Hernandez had volunteered several hours a week in the class, as she was on campus anyway as a part-time paraeducator. Prior to the arrival of students in this new school year, the principal convened a meeting with Ms. Hernandez's special education supervisor, Melony Helprin; the literacy specialist, Wanda Waldrich; the speech and language specialist, Sidia Sooze; and the three classroom teachers. Their task was to determine their roles during BRITE differentiated literacy intervention time and other times during the day. Ms. Prada requested that, after second grade BRITE time, Ms. Hernandez extend her time in Ms. Prada's classroom during the "homeroom" hour of language arts. During this additional hour devoted to literacy, all students receive differentiated language arts instruction. This assignment would allow Ms. Hernandez to help ensure the inclusion of several students eligible for special education in the areas of reading and writing who were Spanish speakers. The team and the principal agreed that this was the best use of Ms. Hernandez's time during this time block.

Third-Grade Team

As shown in Table 2.2, Ms. Hernandez's third-grade team includes the three third-grade teachers: Ms. Rhonda Hart, Ms. Ginny Short, and Mr. Tao Thom. Three others are also included: the special education supervisor, Melony Helprin, the literacy specialist, Wanda Waldrich, and an experienced part-time literacy tutor, Brenda Richards. Ms. Richards has worked with the third-grade classroom teachers for a number of years supporting students who are not eligible for special education but who are not yet proficient on state and district reading and/or mathematics assessments. Being expected this year to also work with students with disabilities is a new role for Ms. Richards. She openly admits that she is worried about her ability to work with a more diverse group of students.

Mr. Thom is the dual immersion teacher for the third-grade level, and this year Ms. Hernandez's daughter is enrolled in his class. Overall, however, the children in his class have lower performance scores in mathematics compared to the other two classes at that grade level. Further, four students with IEPs are included full-time in his class and have IEP goals in mathematics.

When the principal convened the team to make decisions about the roles of the six adults, Ms. Hernandez requested that she not be assigned to Mr. Thom's class, as she felt it might be awkward for her daughter to have her mother teaching in the class. Mr. Thom disagreed, suggesting that Ms. Hernandez and he talk with her daughter about the idea. To Ms. Hernandez's surprise, her daughter was thrilled with the idea of her mother being a co-teacher in her very own class. So, Ms. Hernandez joined

Table 2.2
Members of Ms.
Hernandez's Third-
Grade Team

Name	Role	Responsibilities
Ms. Carlotta Hernandez	5-hour-per-day special education paraeducator	Provides instruction to small groups of students during *BRITE time* and supports classroom teachers during *homeroom* literacy or math instruction
Ms. Suzanne Schmidt	Principal of Chaparral Valley Elementary School	Ensures that *BRITE time* schedules and personnel are delivering instruction and meeting during weekly planning hour
Ms. Rhonda Hart	Third-grade general education teacher	Delivers curriculum and during *BRITE time* provides differentiated instruction to the 20–25 third-grade students with the least need for support in reading instruction
Ms. Ginny Short	Third-grade general education teacher	Delivers curriculum and provides literacy intervention to 20–25 *proficient* third-graders during *BRITE time*
Mr. Tao Thom	Dual immersion third-grade general education teacher	Delivers curriculum and provides literacy intervention for groups of students with some need for additional support in reading instruction during *BRITE time*
Ms. Melony Helprin	Full-time special education teacher	Manages the IEPs for second-, third-, fourth-, and fifth-graders eligible for special education; co-teaches in second- through fourth-grade general education classrooms, and instructs small literacy groups during *BRITE time* for grades 2 through 4
Ms. Wanda Waldrich	Literacy specialist	Supports teachers and students as needed
Ms. Brenda Richards	Experienced part-time literacy tutor	Supports teachers and students as needed

Mr. Thom's class for the math block in order to help bridge students' language and conceptual gaps every day except Wednesdays. On Wednesdays, Ms. Hernandez's special education supervisor, Ms. Helprin, takes her place in the class for the first half of the hour in order to monitor student progress on IEP goals. This arrangement gives Ms. Hernandez time to develop materials and to attend, with the other literacy tutors, the periodic trainings offered by the reading specialist on new literacy materials and programs. For the second half of this math instruction hour, Ms. Hernandez updates Ms. Helprin on the progress data for students with IEPs whom she supports during the second-grade "homeroom" literacy instruction.

■ MEET MS. BARTOLO: THE MIDDLE SCHOOL PARAEDUCATOR AND HER TEAM

All of Ms. Bartolo's own children are now in school, and she recently decided that she wanted to return to work but wanted a job that would allow her to be with her children when they were not in school. She has been hired to work as a paraeducator and has just found out that she is assigned to the middle school. She is eager to begin her new job but is understandably nervous. On her first day of work, Ms. Bartolo is told that she will be assigned to work in the five settings detailed in Table 2.3. After learning about her various responsibilities and meeting with the people with whom she will be working, Ms. Bartolo is even more nervous. She feels some of the people she met were "cold" in their interaction with her and wonders when she will receive training, who will support her, and to whom she will actually report.

Both Ms. Hendrickson and Ms. Cole are veteran English teachers who have been teaching in this middle school for 15 and 11 years, respectively. Although they taught by themselves for the first half of their careers, the increased diversity of the learners they were assigned to teach has resulted in extra adult support being provided in their classrooms. They are experienced in collaborating with special educators, English language learning teachers, paraeducators, and others, and they look forward to working with Ms. Bartolo. In fact, Ms. Bartolo began to feel more at ease when she heard about their experiences working with other paraeducators. For example, she learned that these teachers knew about a study group method that paraeducators can use to learn how to facilitate groups (Fenn, 2005; Fenn & White, 2007).

Table 2.3
Settings and Teachers With Whom Ms. Bartolo Works

Setting	Period	Teacher(s)	Paraeducator Responsibilities
Language Arts 7	1	Ms. Nancy Hendrickson, Language Arts Teacher	General classroom assistant for students with disabilities and others
Language Arts 8	2	Ms. Susan Cole, Language Arts Teacher	General classroom assistant for students with disabilities and others
Science 7	3	Mr. Vun Ruhan, Science Teacher	General classroom assistant for students with disabilities and others
Lunch/Prep	4	N/A	N/A
Learning Center	5	Ms. Deshon Brinkley, Special Education Teacher	1:1 support for student with autism
Special Education Office	6	Ms. Amelia Feldman, Administrative Assistant to the Special Education Director	Clerical

Mr. Ruhan is a first-year science teacher. He has been assigned to teach biology to seventh-graders and physical science to eighth-graders. He has never co-taught, nor has he ever witnessed any of his own teachers co-teaching or working with others in their classroom. He is not pleased about being assigned to work with Ms. Bartolo. Ms. Bartolo overheard him remarking, "I don't know what I'm doing myself; how can I tell her what to do? Assigning her to me is a waste of a resource and a waste of my time." Mr. Ruhan was told when he was hired that the school was implementing inclusive education and that lots of adults were available for meeting, observing, and co-teaching. During orientation he learns that in addition to having Ms. Bartolo in his room, the speech/language therapist, occupational therapist, and the special educator will also be in his room to observe and make recommendations. He is not happy about these "professional visitors," as he feels that they will be there primarily to watch and judge him rather than help him.

Ms. Brinkley, a special education teacher, will be Ms. Bartolo's primary supervisor. Ms. Brinkley is the service coordinator for many of the students with disabilities in the two English classes and one science class as well as Bradley, a young boy with autism, whom Ms. Bartolo will work with in the learning center. Ms. Brinkley has been placed in charge of the learning center, where she creates a generic environment where any student can receive short- or long-term support on an as-needed basis. Some students (e.g., Bradley) will be assigned to the learning center for one period daily. Other students can self-refer or be referred by a teacher for short-term assistance. Ms. Brinkley also is coordinating a cross-age peer-tutoring program. By the second semester, peer tutors will be available in the learning center to support fellow students. Ms. Brinkley informs Ms. Bartolo that Bradley's parents are very involved with his program and will want frequent communication about how he is doing; Ms. Brinkley warns Ms. Bartolo to be careful in the communication as it should come primarily from her, Ms. Brinkley. She tells Ms. Bartolo that the school is a little leery of the family because they have filed legal due process complaints against the school in the past.

Ms. Feldman has been an administrative assistant to the special education director for five years. The director's office is housed in the middle school. Ms. Feldman has been told that Ms. Bartolo will report to the office to assist with clerical responsibilities the last period of the day. She is a little puzzled to learn this, as this will be the first time such help has been made available and it comes as a surprise. In speaking with Ms. Brinkley, Ms. Feldman learns that it may be short-term until they identify another instructional duty for Ms. Bartolo. Ms. Brinkley tells Ms. Feldman, "We didn't know what to do with her during that period, so we assigned her to you."

MEET MR. ANDERSON: THE SECONDARY SCHOOL PARAEDUCATOR AND HIS TEAM ■

Mr. Anderson is beginning his fourth year as a paraeducator working at the secondary level. Mr. Anderson is studying evenings and summers at the university and hopes to obtain his teaching certification within two years. He very much enjoys his work at the high school and the team of 10th-grade general and special educators with whom he has worked for the past three years. He feels that he has learned more about teaching with these professionals than he has in his coursework at the university. Mr. Anderson is grateful for the once-monthly and two-day summer training sessions provided to the paraeducators in the district. In addition, although not compensated for attending, he is permitted to attend training seminars provided to the professional staff. He has attended training on inclusive education, cooperative group learning, co-teaching, positive behavioral supports, and differentiation of instruction. The settings and people with whom Mr. Anderson works are depicted in Table 2.4. Mr. Anderson, Mr. Schwab, Ms. Bennevento, and Ms. Clooney form the team. The professional staff meets four days a week for 20 minutes at the start of the day. Mr. Anderson joins them on two of the four days. Typically, Mr. Anderson co-teaches with Mr. Schwab or Ms. Bennevento when Ms. Clooney, the special educator, is with the other teacher. For example, when Ms. Clooney is with Mr. Schwab, Mr. Anderson is with Ms. Bennevento. Occasionally, due to the nature of the lesson or the level of support needed by some students, both Ms. Clooney and Mr. Anderson may be in the same general education classroom. The decision as to how to allocate human resources for the upcoming week is always decided upon collaboratively at the weekly Thursday meeting that all team members, including Mr. Anderson, attend.

Mr. Schwab is a veteran science teacher who also serves as chair of the science department. He has taught in the district for 32 years. Although eligible for retirement, he has decided to teach for another 5 years because, as he says, "I'm having too much fun and learning too many new strategies to quit." He is popular among staff and students. Mr. Schwab is delighted to have additional support in his classroom as well as a collaborative planning team that provides support to him through brainstorming and sharing. He has been co-teaching with Ms. Clooney and Mr. Anderson for three years—he feels that they just keep getting better at what they do.

Ms. Bennevento arrived in the United States four years ago. She is a native of Italy. Ms. Bennevento had prior experience including students with disabilities and with co-teaching in Italy. Although initially uncomfortable with the American system of education, she has adjusted and is enjoying her work. She feels comfortable with her team and would like to keep it together. Ms. Bennevento strongly encourages Mr. Anderson to complete his studies so that he can receive his certification and earn a better wage as a teacher. She plans to return to Italy in two to three years, when her husband completes his doctoral program in engineering.

Ms. Clooney began her educational career as a paraeducator. She is a veteran special educator of 13 years. Ms. Clooney changed jobs and came to this high school 5 years ago. She had taught in her previous secondary school placement for 7 years. For the first 4 years of her teaching career she taught in a "pull out" resource room program. Her district adopted a more inclusive approach and she found herself "pushing into" general education classrooms during her fifth and sixth year working in that district. Although a little reluctant at first, she soon cherished her role as a co-teacher and saw tremendous benefits for her students who were placed in

Setting	Period/ Block	Teacher	Paraeducator Responsibilities
Ms. Bennevento's classroom Monday Mr. Schwab's classroom Thursday	Before School	Mr. Schwab Ms. Bennevento Ms. Clooney	Attend twice-weekly (Monday and Thursday) 20-minute meeting before school with all team members
Science Social Studies	1	Mr. Schwab M, W, F Ms. Bennevento T, TH	Check homework, monitor cooperative groups, record information on smart board or overhead transparencies, add words to the Word Wall, parallel co-teach at stations
		Ms. Clooney and other paraeducators	Attend once-monthly paraeducator training sessions held during first block
Social Studies Science	2	Ms. Bennevento M, W, F Mr. Schwab T, TH	Check homework, monitor cooperative groups, record information on smart board or overhead transparencies, add words to the Word Wall, parallel co-teach at stations
Planning Social Studies Science	3	Ms. Clooney W Ms. Bennevento M, W, F Mr. Schwab T, TH	Meet with for first 20 minutes of class on Wednesday. Check homework, monitor cooperative groups, record information on smart board or overhead transparencies, add words to the Word Wall, parallel co-teach at stations
Lunch 20 minutes daily	N/A	N/A	N/A
Individual Planning 15 minutes daily	N/A	N/A	Develop materials and/or review materials
Science Social Studies	4	Mr. Schwab M, W, F Ms. Bennevento T, TH	Check homework, monitor cooperative groups, record information on smart board or overhead transparencies, add words to the Word Wall, parallel co-teach at stations

Table 2.4
Settings and Teachers With Whom Mr. Anderson Works

the general education classrooms. Her sixth year of teaching resulted in a return to pullout, as the administration changed and favored that approach. Dissatisfied with a return to pullout services, Ms. Clooney applied for and was hired to work in this new high school. For the past three years, she has been co-teaching with Mr. Anderson, Mr. Schwab, and Ms. Bennevento. She says, "These past three years have been the best years of my career!" She is looking forward to her fourth year of co-teaching with these valued colleagues.

■ SUMMARY

At the beginning of this chapter you were asked the following questions:

- What do you believe will be the paraeducators' greatest challenges when they begin to work together?
- How are the paraeducators' work situations similar or different to your own work situation or the situations of the paraeducators who work in your school?
- If you were the paraeducator for each of the three teams described in this book, what aspects of your situation would you perceive as positive or supportive?
- If you were the paraeducator in any of the three teams, what questions or concerns would you want to discuss with your supervisor or team members?

Now that you have "met" Ms. Hernandez, the elementary-level paraeducator; Ms. Bartolo, the middle school paraeducator; and Mr. Anderson, the high school paraeducator, how would you answer each of those questions? In what ways can you identify with these three paraeducators? Do you detect the positive aspects of their positions? Do you identify that each of the paraeducators must face unique challenges? How are their work situations similar to or different from one another or similar to or different from your own work situation? What issues do you believe need to be raised with any of the paraeducators' teams or supervisors?

Were you able to identify some of the challenges that these paraeducators might face? For example, there might be challenges with respect to the time involved for the paraeducators to learn the new content they might need to teach the grade-level material to students with and without disabilities. Another challenge might be that the paraeducators will need to learn time management skills to make sure they show up in the various classrooms to which they are assigned. Still another challenge might involve feelings of intimidation due to all that must be learned! And, a challenge faced by many paraeducators—similar to what Ms. Bartolo might face—is working with teachers who don't know what to do with them!

Were you able to detect the supportive aspects of each scenario? For example, Ms. Hernandez was invited to participate in the professional development experiences to learn about Response to Intervention techniques. Would you find that to be supportive? Similarly, co-teachers who helped her access resources to assist with her assignment guided Ms. Bartolo. How similar or different are these situations compared to your own?

Now that you have entered the worlds of these three paraeducators, let's examine their roles and responsibilities in each of their job situations. As you read through the next chapter, think about how you can apply what you are learning about Ms. Hernandez, Ms. Bartolo, and Mr. Anderson.

Redefining the Roles and Responsibilities of Paraeducators

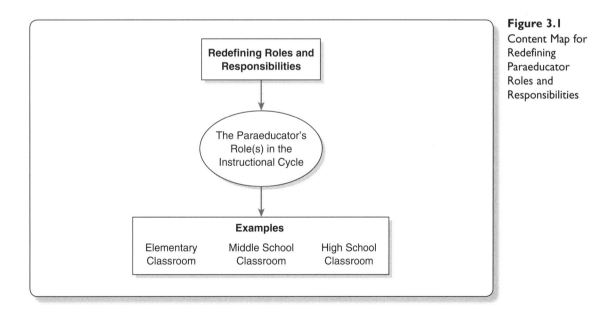

Figure 3.1
Content Map for Redefining Paraeducator Roles and Responsibilities

This chapter will provide answers to the following questions:

1. What roles and responsibilities do paraeducators take on when they work in inclusive classrooms?

2. What are the different roles and responsibilities for others, such as classroom teachers, when they work with paraeducators in inclusive classrooms?

3. What are paraeducator roles in the instructional cycle?

■ THE VARIETY OF ROLES AND RESPONSIBILITIES THAT PARAEDUCATORS TAKE ON WHEN THEY WORK IN INCLUSIVE SCHOOLS

Paraeducators take on many diverse roles. The literature on the day-to-day work of paraeducators is clear about the differentiated roles that paraeducators can and do perform. As described in Chapter 1, paraeducators are key players with classroom teachers who differentiate instruction through co-teaching and other techniques. Table 3.1 summarizes the varied roles that appear in the literature, including note taker, behavioral aide, teacher/translator, communicator, tutor, bilingual aide, and co-teacher under the supervision of general education teachers.

Table 3.1
Documented Roles of Paraeducators in Inclusive Schools

Role	Source
Co-teacher in general education classrooms	Villa, Thousand, and Nevin (2008a, 2008b, 2008c)
Teacher for reading, math, and writing to small groups	Ashbaker & Morgan (2001)
Supervises students working in cooperative learning groups and as peer tutors	Nevin, Malian, et al. (2007)
Teacher and translator for children who speak languages other than English	Wenger et al. (2004)
Teacher of pro-social behavior (sharing)	Perez & Murdock (1999)
Behavioral aide for students with autism	Young (1997)
Note taker in general education classes for students with hearing impairment	Yarger (1996)
Speech-language assistant	Radaszewski-Byrne (1997)
Aide for bilingual learners	Ashbaker & Morgan (2000)
Communicator between Native American families of children with disabilities and school personnel	Ashbaker & Morgan (2001)
Playground aide, materials preparation, tutorials	Nevin, Cramer, et al. (2007)

THE DIFFERENT ROLES AND RESPONSIBILITIES ■
FOR OTHERS WHEN THEY WORK WITH
PARAEDUCATORS IN INCLUSIVE CLASSROOMS

How do you decide a paraeducator's role? Paraeducators and their teachers are encouraged to clearly articulate what the paraeducator's role should be. The first recommendation to school districts and states is "to have a clear definition of the paraprofessional's role in the classroom and the related roles of the teacher and administrator" (Torrence-Mikulecky & Baber, 2005, p. 1). Role clarification can be complex, because a paraeducator's role may change dramatically throughout the course of a school day depending upon the changing needs of students and the decisions made by the professional educators who collectively decide the specifics of the job in each instructional situation. At least the following areas need to be clarified: (a) lesson planning, (b) delivery of instruction, (c) proactive and reactive responses to students' behaviors, (d) strategies to promote ongoing communication, and (e) methods of student evaluation (Doyle, 2002). Two other areas might include confidentiality and team participation (French, 2008a, 2008b). Later in this chapter, we show how a paraeducator's team might use the roles and responsibilities matrix (see Table 3.5 and Resource A). The matrix guides decisions on specific roles, depending on the needs of the diverse students in the classroom and the skills and expertise of the co-teaching team members (including the paraeducator).

Remember that the job of the paraeducator is to *supplement* the instruction of qualified teaching professionals under the direction of those professionals. In other words, it is the professional educator, not the paraeducator, who is to take the lead in developing and directing the delivery of curriculum, instruction, and student assessments (French, 2008b). We all are encouraged to be clear about who will supervise paraeducators in inclusive settings, especially within a collaborative team approach (Pickett & Gerlach, 2003). Such clarification of role and responsibilities is important because the No Child Left Behind Act specifies that paraeducators who provide instruction in Title I–funded programs must provide services under the direct supervision of a highly qualified teacher (Title I, Section 1119(g)(2)).

There are two excellent national resources to assist paraeducators and their team members in clarifying the role of paraeducators and developing useful job descriptions. One is the PAR^{2}A Center (www.para center.org) and the other is the National Resource Center for Paraprofessionals (www.nrcpara.org).

PARAEDUCATOR ROLES ■
IN THE INSTRUCTIONAL CYCLE

To help paraeducators understand their roles in the instructional cycle, we begin by describing how teachers think about the instructional cycle. Teachers engage in an ongoing recursive instructional cycle shown in Figure 3.2. They go through this cycle when developing, delivering, and reflecting on their instruction.

First, as shown in the figure, teachers *plan*. They plan their units and lessons. Planning includes getting to know the students in the class, the content that is to be delivered and the state standards that the content addresses, and what students are expected to know or do and how this will be assessed, as well as what experiences will be constructed to help students make sense of the content.

Then, teachers *deliver* or *implement* the planned lesson. While they are doing this, they monitor and adjust their instruction during the lesson as they observe and collect anecdotal or more formal information on how students are responding to what they have planned. Finally, after the lesson, teachers reflect on the lesson and evaluate how successful it was in achieving the intended learning outcomes for the students.

Paraeducators in co-taught classrooms may be called upon to assist in instruction at any point of the instructional cycle. They may be asked to plan, teach, monitor student progress, collect data, and reflect upon and evaluate instruction; this may be done at the individual student level or for all of the students in a classroom.

When paraeducators assist in the planning point of the cycle, they often are asked to assist teachers to adapt what typically has occurred in a classroom in order to allow a student who learns differently to access the general education curriculum. In order to be able to determine what to adapt, educators must have information about both the learning characteristics of a student of concern and the characteristics of classroom instruction. This requires gathering data about the student and data about the content, product, and process demands of the classrooms.

Figure 3.2
The Instructional
Cycle

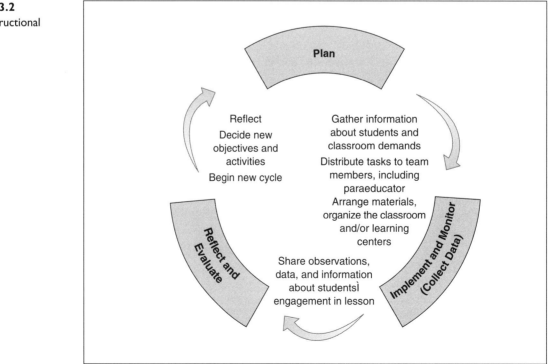

Addressing Mismatches Between Student Characteristics and Classroom Demands

Often, when students are struggling, paraeducators as well as the educators they assist may be tempted to focus upon and gather information primarily about students' perceived deficits. They either ignore or downplay information about what students do well and under what conditions they perform best. Instead, we suggest a strengths-based perspective. This begins with gathering information about students' strengths, learning preferences or styles, multiple intelligences, and interests as well as the demands of the classroom. This is the first step in determining how to develop adaptations that use and build upon student characteristics and strengths.

Figure 3.3 offers a template that paraeducators and teachers can use to gather information as a starting point for discovering and addressing mismatches between a student's characteristics and typical classroom demands (also see Resource B). The left-hand side of the template first prompts the discovery of *positive* student information as well as specific student goals and needs. The right-hand side of the template prompts planners to examine the content, product/assessment, and process/ instructional dimensions of the typical demands of the classroom.

Student Characteristics	Classroom Demands
Strengths	**Content Demands**
Background Knowledge and Experiences	How is the content made available to the learners?
Interests	What multi-level materials are used?
Learning Style(s)	
Multiple Intelligences	**Process Demands**
Important Relationships	What processes or instructional methods do the co-teachers use to facilitate student learning?
Other: _____	
Other: _____	
Goals	**Product Demands**
Does this learner have any unique goals related to academic learning, communication, English language acquisition, and/or social-emotional functioning?	How do the students demonstrate what they have learned?
	How are students assessed or graded?
Are there particular concerns about this learner?	

Figure 3.3

Template for Gathering Information About Student Characteristics and Classroom Demands

The next step in the process of crafting adaptations is to compare the student and classroom information included in Figure 3.3 in order to identify mismatches between the two. It may be discovered that there is mismatch between how the student accesses content and the typical materials used (i.e., content demands). For example, a seventh-grade student reading at a fourth-grade level may have only seventh-grade-level textbooks available in the classroom. This represents a *materials* mismatch. There may be a mismatch between how the student best shows what he or she knows and how students typically are assessed. This is a *product* mismatch. There may be a mismatch between how the student best acquires knowledge or skills and how instruction typically has occurred. This would be a *process* mismatch.

Armed with information about these identified mismatches, a team then can collaboratively consider possible ways to provide support or change the task demands—the content and material (content demands), how the student is asked to show what he or she knows (product demands), and/or what is done during instruction (process demands). Because paraeducators are assisting other educational personnel—classroom teachers, special educators, teachers of English language learners—they have many people with various knowledge bases and experiences with whom they can brainstorm solutions to mismatches.

When generating potential solutions, it is important to avoid solutions that might lead to stigmatization of a student. Thus, we suggest whatever you consider as a possible solution for a mismatch for a struggling student also should be considered and made available to any student who might benefit. We further suggest that when prioritizing solutions to mismatches, a team first consider solutions that meet at least the three following criteria:

1. The solution is the least intrusive—least likely to disrupt what goes on in the classroom with all of the other students.

2. The solution is only as special as necessary; that is, you do not over-support a student.

3. The solution is the most natural (e.g., natural peer supports, use of already-existing technology) to the context of the classroom.

To support the brainstorming process, we suggest that paraeducators and teachers use Resource C of this book, "A Checklist of Sample Supplemental Supports, Aids, and Services." This comprehensive checklist offers paraeducators and the educators they assist a broad range of options for supports, aids, services, adaptations, and so forth that can meet the "least intrusive," "only as special as necessary," and "most natural" criteria.

With this information about the instructional cycle, strategies, and tools for adapting instruction through comparing information about students and typical classroom demands, let's delve into the day-to-day workings of the paraeducators you met in Chapter 2. Let's discover how their diverse roles are developing and how their roles are engaging them in the instructional cycle.

MS. HERNANDEZ: ELEMENTARY PARAEDUCATOR ROLES AND RESPONSIBILITIES

We learned in Chapter 2 that Ms. Hernandez now is a member of both second- and third-grade teams that include the school principal, the general education teachers at each grade level, the full-time special education teacher, the reading specialist for the second-grade team, the speech and language specialist, and a paraeducator who previously has served as a third-grade literacy tutor. Ms. Hernandez met the formal job description requirements for the Special Education Instructional Assistant Level I for which she was hired. The four-page job description is a laundry list of representative duties, most of which sounded much like the instructional duties of a classroom teacher.

In order to qualify for this job, Ms. Hernandez had to have an updated first aid certificate and a cardiopulmonary resuscitation (CPR) certificate. Because this was a school that received Title I, Part A funds, she needed to meet the No Child Left Behind requirements for new paraeducators: Namely, she had to pass a district subject matter examination that showed she had the knowledge to assist in instructing in reading, writing, and mathematics. The alternative ways to qualify for the job were to hold an associate's degree, have two years (48 credit hours) of university-level study, or one year of experience plus a child development course. She did not have this training or experience, but fortunately, she passed the district's examination.

A new feature of this school year was the establishment of a 1.5-hour block of time to differentiate language arts instruction for the second through fifth grades. This *differentiated literacy time* supplements each classroom teacher's hour or so of "homeroom" reading and language arts instruction.

During the previous year, the kindergarten and first-grade teachers had already joined forces for literacy instruction. Their approach was to have students stay in their own classrooms and have the school's literacy tutors come into the classroom to join the classroom teachers to provide targeted small group instruction. The literacy tutors, funded through Title I dollars, are under the direct supervision of the literacy specialist and special educators. The K–1 team, including the specialists and tutors, meets weekly to plan interventions. This includes the implementation of the district's Reading Recovery intervention for the lowest-achieving first-graders (see the Web site of the Reading Recovery Council of America for a description).

This is the school's and the district's first experiment with blending instructional resources school-wide in order to tailor instruction to students based upon need rather than label (i.e., general education, special education, Title I), in accordance with Response to Intervention (RtI) principles articulated in the 2004 reauthorization of the Individuals with Disabilities Educational Improvement Act (IDEIA). The school has 1.5 hours of *differentiated literacy group time* four days a week (exclusive of Wednesday) in second through fifth grades. The faculty named this time Block

Reading Intervention Toward Excellence (BRITE) time, because the name and acronym seem to capture the spirit of their effort. During BRITE time, every person in the school becomes an *intervention educator* and students are regrouped into intervention groups across same-grade classrooms. Students are assigned to small groups based upon their assessed performance on the various dimensions of literacy (i.e., phonemic awareness, phonics, fluency, vocabulary, and text comprehension). Weekly, during Wednesday noontime planning meetings, grade-level teams examine student performance and fluidly move students among instructional groups based upon each student's progress or lack of progress.

Table 3.2 (page 33-34) shows the 8:00 a.m. to 1:15 p.m. work schedule for Ms. Hernandez and her teammates and lays out her daily schedule for the four days a week of the BRITE *differentiated literacy group time*. Classrooms in the school are physically clustered by grade level. There are three classes per grade level, with 60 to 75 students per grade on average. The BRITE time is staggered across the grades so that support personnel (i.e., special education teachers and paraeducators, literacy specialist and tutors, speech and language specialist) can rotate through each grade level's BRITE time.

Ms. Hernandez's second- and third-grade teams met and agreed that the BRITE *differentiated literacy group time* would be the first hour (i.e., 8:15–9:15 a.m.) of the day, while the third-grade team would have the hour of *homeroom* literacy during this time frame. Support personnel then could rotate into the third-grade BRITE intervention block at 9:20 a.m. When students and instructors regroup for BRITE time, the classroom teachers generally stay in their classrooms, and the other support personnel (i.e., special educator, paraeducator, reading specialist, literacy tutor) are distributed across the classrooms. Tables 3.3 and 3.4 show how the second- and third-grade teams distribute their resources.

Ms. Hernandez's Second-Grade Team

In second grade, Ms. Hernandez and two other support personnel join Mr. Drumming to form a four-person team; each takes a group of three to eight students, based upon the intensity and type of literacy instruction needed to support various students. The speech and language specialist usually teaches the students who need intensive instruction in phonemic awareness and decoding. Students in this classroom often rotate among instructors to receive instruction on different dimensions of literacy (e.g., text comprehension, fluency, phonics). The reading specialist and the dual immersion second-grade teacher teach a group of students who need less intensive support and strategically group and regroup students during the BRITE period. Ms. Dahl teaches the students who are performing well across the literacy spectrum and uses a combination of large group, individual, and station learning situations to differentiate instruction for this larger group of students.

Table 3.2

Daily Schedule, Curriculum Focus, and Responsibilities for Ms. Hernandez's Teams

Time Period	Curriculum Focus	Team Members	Team Member Responsibilities
8:00–8:15 a.m.	Class meetings in all classrooms for all grade levels	Classroom teachers hold daily class meetings with their class of students.	Ms. Hernandez does not begin work until 8:15 but is available for employment for extra duties, if needed (e.g., tutorial, playground support).
8:15–9:15 a.m.	Second-grade literacy *BRITE time* Note: Students in smaller groups often rotate among instructors and interventions focusing upon different dimensions of literacy (e.g., comprehension, phonemic awareness).	Ms. Robin Dahl, second-grade teacher	Instructs 20–25 highest-performing second-graders
		Ms. Suyapa Prada, dual immersion second-grade teacher	Instructs 5–10 second-graders with some need for additional support
		Ms. Hernandez, paraeducator	Instructs 5–10 second-graders with some need for additional support
		Mr. Tim Drumming, second-grade teacher	Instructs 3–8 second-graders with great need
		Ms. Melony Helprin, special educator	Instructs 3–8 second-graders with great need
		Ms. Wanda Waldrich, reading specialist	Instructs 3–8 second-graders with great need
		Ms. Sidia Sooze, speech and language specialist	Instructs 3–8 second-graders with great need
9:20–10:20 a.m.	Third-grade literacy *BRITE time* Note: Students in smaller groups often rotate among instructors and interventions focusing upon different dimensions of literacy (e.g., comprehension, phonemic awareness).	Ms. Rhonda Hart, third-grade teacher	Instructs 20–25 highest-performing third-graders
		Ms. Ginny Short, third-grade teacher	Instructs 5–10 third-graders with some need for additional support
		Ms. Wanda Waldrich, reading specialist	Instructs 5–10 third-graders with some need for additional support
		Mr. Toa Thom, dual immersion third-grade teacher	Instructs 3–8 third-graders with great need
		Ms. Melony Helprin, special educator	Instructs 3–8 third-graders with great need
		Ms. Brenda Richards, literacy tutor	Instructs 3–8 third-graders with great need
		Ms. Hernandez, paraeducator	Instructs 3–8 third-graders with great need
10:30–11:30 a.m.	Second-grade literacy "homeroom" instruction	Ms. Suyapa Prada, dual immersion second-grade teacher Ms. Hernandez, paraeducator	General classroom literacy instruction with a focus upon differentiating for students with disabilities and English learners

Table 3.2 (Continued)

Time Period	Curriculum Focus	Team Members	Team Member Responsibilities
11:40 a.m.–12:40 p.m.	Third-grade mathematics instruction	Mr. Toa Thom, dual immersion third-grade teacher Ms. Hernandez, paraeducator	General classroom mathematics instruction; focus on differentiation for students with disabilities, English learners, and others below proficient in math
12:45–1:15 p.m.	Lunch and plan time (Monday, Tuesday, Thursday, Friday)	Ms. Melony Helprin, special educator Ms. Hernandez, paraeducator	Individual education program (IEP) monitoring and data sharing
Noon–1:15 p.m. Wednesday	Weekly Wednesday Lunch Hour Meetings	Joins second-grade team for *team time* data analysis and planning for the first 30 minutes; joins third-grade team for *team time* data analysis and planning for second 30 minutes. (The other 30 minutes of the lunch hour are devoted to other grade-level curriculum discussions.) Suzanne Schmidt, principal, attends each grade level's *team time* meeting at least biweekly; extended problem solving or preparation time (1:00–1:15).	

As shown in Table 3.4, the third-grade BRITE period is structured similar to that of the second grade. At third grade, Ms. Hernandez is with Mr. Thom, the dual immersion teacher who, with the help of Ms. Hernandez, her supervising special educator, and a literacy tutor, provides small group instruction to the students with greatest need.

Table 3.3
Second-Grade BRITE Differentiated Literacy Group Time

Time Period	Ms. Robin Dahl, Classroom Teacher	Ms. Suyapa Prada, Dual Immersion Teacher	Mr. Tim Drumming, Classroom Teacher
8:15–9:15 a.m. (60 minutes)	Population: Students with least need for support in reading instruction (20–25 students)	Population: Students with some need for additional support in reading instruction (15–20 students, 2 educators, 5–10 students per group) Additional Support: Reading Specialist (Ms. Wanda Waldrich)	Population: Students in great need for support in reading instruction (25–30 students, 3 educators, 3–8 students per educator with smaller groups for students with most intensive needs) Additional Support: Special Educator (Ms. Melony Helprin) Speech and Language Specialist (Ms. Sidia Sooze) Paraeducator (Ms. Hernandez)

Table 3.4

Third-Grade BRITE Differentiated Literacy Group Time

Time Period	Ms. Rhonda Hart, Classroom Teacher	Mr. Tao Thom, Dual Immersion Classroom Teacher	Ms. Ginny Short, Classroom Teacher
9:20–10:20 a.m. (60 minutes)	Population: Students with least need for support in reading instruction (20–25 students)	Population: Students with some need for additional support in reading instruction (15–20 students, 2 educators, 5–10 students per group) Additional Support: Paraeducator (Ms. Hernandez)	Population: Students in great need of support in reading instruction (25–30 students, 3 educators, 3–8 students per educator, with smaller groups for students with most intensive needs) Additional Support: Special Educator (Ms. Melony Helprin) Reading Specialist (Ms. Wanda Waldrich) Literacy Tutor (Ms. Brenda Richards) Paraeducator (Ms. Hernandez)

MS. BARTOLO: ■
MIDDLE SCHOOL PARAEDUCATOR
ROLES AND RESPONSIBILITIES

During her first three weeks of employment, Ms. Bartolo wondered many times whether she had made a mistake in accepting the paraeducator position. Ms. Brinkley—the special educator and her supervisor—though nice to her, seems too overwhelmed by her own numerous and varied responsibilities to provide the direction, training, and support Ms. Bartolo feels she needs and deserves. Ms. Bartolo has asked Ms. Brinkley for a job description on three separate occasions. Each time she mentions it, Ms. Brinkley replies that she is in the process of developing it. Ms. Bartolo likes Ms. Brinkley and realizes how hard she is working. Ms. Bartolo does not want to be an additional burden for her. Nonetheless, Ms. Bartolo is unsure of her responsibilities. She wonders whether she is doing the "right" thing in her work, especially in the science class and in working with Bradley, a student with autism.

Although both Ms. Brinkley and Ms. Bartolo are in the learning center at the same time during fifth period, Ms. Brinkley appears busy, as she is training and working with peer tutors at that time and is not available to meet with or supervise Ms. Bartolo. Ms. Bartolo has been assigned to work with Bradley in the learning center. Ms. Bartolo is given a folder with work for Bradley to do during this time. She especially wonders how to respond to Bradley when he appears to zone out, refuses to work, rocks in his chair, and repeats several times things that he overhears other students saying. She is unsure whether his refusal to do work is because he cannot do the work or because he is testing her. Bradley and Ms. Bartolo sit at the back of the learning center, as far away from the other students and adults as possible, so as not to disturb them.

Mr. Ruhan, the science teacher, does not appear to have "warmed up" to Ms. Bartolo. He still seems cold and distant. When she asked him what he would like her to do in his class, he said, "I don't know. Didn't they tell you?" He seems to get distracted if she moves around the room to help students while he is lecturing. After the first week, he told her to sit in the last seat of the first row and take notes to give to the students with individual education programs (IEPs) who do not appear able to keep up with his rapid pace of the lesson. This week, he told her to continue to do that but first to make copies of the materials he places in the basket with her name on it. Each day this week, Ms. Bartolo was given so many things to copy, she missed more than half of the class period. To be honest, she does not mind missing the class, as Mr. Ruhan is having numerous behavior problems with the students in the class and frequently responds by yelling at the students.

Although her clerical duties during the last period of the day in the special education office are routine and easy for Ms. Bartolo, she would prefer to work with students. She wishes she could spend more time in either Ms. Hendrickson's or Ms. Cole's language arts classes. Working with them is the highlight of her day and the reason she has not quit her job. The three of them eat lunch together, and they both have been very clear about Ms. Bartolo's responsibilities in their classes. Together with Ms. Bartolo, they complete the role and responsibilities matrix that appears in Table 3.5. Having worked with Ms. Brinkley and other paraeducators in the past, they are familiar with the role that paraeducators usually assume in supporting the students assigned to their classes.

A blank copy of the Co-Teaching Roles and Responsibilities Matrix appears in the Resources section of this book (see Resource A).

Both Ms. Hendrickson and Ms. Cole have told Ms. Bartolo that they like it when she circulates among the students and supports any learner who appears to be struggling. They told her that her primary responsibility is to facilitate independence and peer interdependence rather than becoming Velcroed to any child or fostering a sense of co-dependence. They have modeled for her how to turn problems back to the students and how to facilitate peer interactions. Based on her own experiences supporting students with disabilities in this classroom, Ms. Bartolo is becoming increasingly uncomfortable about how she and Bradley have become an "island" unto themselves within the learning center.

Ms. Bartolo shares with Ms. Hendrickson and Ms. Cole her concerns about not having a job description and the dynamic in her work with Bradley in the learning center and with Mr. Ruhan in the science class. Ms. Hendrickson and Ms. Cole tell Ms. Bartolo that they need to think about her situation and promise to share some ideas on the following day. When next they meet, they tell Ms. Bartolo that they are very pleased with her work in their classes. They explain that, as time goes by and her confidence and skill level increase, they plan to expand her co-teaching from just the supportive role to sometimes running a parallel group and doing complementary things like recording on the board or overhead while they teach. Ms. Bartolo is excited to hear how her instructional role will expand in the future as she gains new skills.

Table 3.5

Co-Teaching Roles and Responsibilities Matrix

Responsibilities	Ms. Bartolo, Paraeducator	Ms. Cole, Language Arts Teacher	Ms. Hendrickson, Language Arts Teacher	Ms. Brinkley, Special Educator
Develop units, projects, lessons	I	P	P	I
Instruct students	S	P	P	I
Monitor student progress	E	E	E	E
Assign grades	I	P	P	S
Create advance organizers	S	P	P	
Note-taking, model use of graphic organizers	E	E	E	
Facilitate peer support, friendships	E	P	P	I
Discipline/behavior management	S	P	P	I
Communicate with parents	S	E	E	E
Develop IEPs	I	S	S	P
Communicate with administrators	S	P	P	P
Attend team meetings	E	E	E	E
Train paraeducator		S	S	P
Supervise paraeducator		E	E	E

KEY: P = Primary Responsibility; S = Secondary Responsibility; E = Equal Responsibility; I = Input

Ms. Cole and Ms. Hendrickson share their opinion that if no job description is forthcoming, perhaps Ms. Bartolo should prepare one and share it with Ms. Brinkley for her review and comment. Ms. Bartolo voices the concern that she is not sure that she would know what to put in a job description. They tell her that they both are available to assist her in developing one, and Ms. Cole refers Ms. Bartolo to the Web site to learn about job-embedded professional development study groups for paraeducators. Ms. Bartolo emphasized how impressed she had been with the paraprofessionals she knew in Connecticut who had participated in the study groups (Fenn, 2005; Fenn & White, 2007).

> For information on study groups, see http://paraconnect.com/ColorMeSuccessful.html.

With respect to Mr. Ruhan's class, Ms. Hendrickson and Ms. Cole suggest that Ms. Bartolo "sit tight" for a while to see whether things improve. They suggest that if in a month there is no improvement, she should ask for a meeting with Ms. Brinkley and Mr. Ruhan and ask to be transferred elsewhere if Mr. Ruhan is unable at that time to find a more productive role for her. They volunteer to attend the meeting as well and share how they are working with her in their classes. As an alternative to meeting with her supervisor, they suggest that after she creates the draft job description based on what she is currently and will be doing in their classes and reviews the material on the Web site, she meet with Mr. Ruhan and present it to him and begin to plan how her role can change in his class.

Ms. Bartolo is feeling much better and has one more concern that she wishes to discuss with the two English teachers. She is worried about her work with Bradley, especially because Bradley's mother has stopped her twice already as she was leaving school to discuss his program and progress in the learning center. Ms. Hendrickson suggests that Ms. Bartolo share that information with Ms. Brinkley and request that Ms. Brinkley model for her how to work with Bradley and respond to the behaviors that she finds puzzling. Ms. Bartolo is thrilled with their support and ideas and plans to implement every one of their recommendations.

■ MR. ANDERSON: SECONDARY SCHOOL PARAEDUCATOR ROLES AND RESPONSIBILITIES

The detailed paraeducator job description presented to Mr. Anderson at his orientation appears in Table 3.6. Ms. Clooney, the special education teacher, reviewed the job description with him at that time and has reviewed it with him twice since then. Mr. Anderson learned that although Ms. Clooney is his formal supervisor, Mr. Schwab and Ms. Bennevento would also provide input into his formal evaluation. Mr. Anderson is not worried about his formal evaluation because all three of his teammates provide him with constructive feedback on a weekly basis, and they have been working well together for over three years.

Table 3.6
Paraeducator Position Description

Title:	Paraeducator
Department:	Special Education
Report to:	Supervisor, Classroom Teachers, and Principal
Position Summary:	Paraeducator works with individual and small groups of students in classroom and other instructional settings to provide specially designed instruction in conjunction with classroom teachers, special educators, related service providers, and other members of the school community.
Essential Functions:	Accepts responsibility for being a member of a collegial group. Assists teacher with implementation of Individualized Education Programs. Assists in the preparation of a variety of instructional materials and learning aids; rephrases directions and materials.

Essential Functions (Continued):	Assists students in completing classroom assignments, homework, and projects in various subject areas. Assists students by answering questions, providing proper examples, emotional support, friendly attitude, and general guidance. Tutors individual students or groups of students. Regularly administers placement, achievement, and diagnostic tests or other special program tests and records data. Collects and records behavioral data. Implements assigned sections of pupil behavior management plans. Performs a variety of clerical duties such as preparing, typing, and duplicating instructional materials. Maintains the confidentiality of student records and information. Provides support to instructional personnel by setting up work areas, displays, and exhibits. Maintains classroom environment in a safe, clean, and orderly condition. Ensures health and safety of students by following health and safety practices and procedures. Participates in staff meetings, inservice training, and parent and student conferences as assigned. Performs other related duties as assigned.
Knowledge of:	Child guidance principles and practices. Problems and concerns of students with special needs. General subjects taught such as mathematics, reading, writing, English, history, science. Basic instructional methods. Correct English usage, grammar, spelling, punctuation, and vocabulary. Oral and written communication skills. Interpersonal skills. Basic record-keeping skills.
Ability to:	Provide instructional support and assistance to teachers and students assigned to a designated special education program. Assist with instruction and related activities in a classroom or assigned learning environment. Perform instructional support activities related to behavior management. Reinforce instruction to students with disabilities. Understand and follow oral and written directions. Establish and maintain collaborative working relationship with others. Maintain confidentiality.
Education and Experience:	Pass district examination for this position or complete 48 college/university semester units or equivalent quarter units and complete coursework in child development related to students with disabilities. Complete one-year experience working with students of various age levels requiring a specialized learning environment.
License and Other Requirements	Valid First Aid and CPR certificates issued by an authorized agency

■ **SUMMARY**

To what extent did you discover your own answers to the questions posed at the beginning of the chapter? You've learned about the wide range of roles that paraeducators can take on when they work in inclusive classrooms. You've learned about how teachers think about the instructional cycle and how paraeducators might fit into that cycle. You have peeked into the day-to-day workings of paraeducators like Ms. Hernandez, Ms. Bartolo, and Mr. Anderson, and you have learned how their school days have been organized. You have also learned what researchers and other experts say about roles and responsibilities, and you have seen how the three teaching teams have varied in the way they included supervision and professional development within their busy schedules. Some of the classroom teachers and other specialists have also changed their roles and responsibilities to make sure that the paraeducators can do their work more effectively.

In Chapter 4, you will discover more about the collaborative planning process. You will detect effective strategies that paraeducators and other members of co-teaching teams can use to get the most out of their collaborative planning.

Collaborative Processes

Tips and Strategies

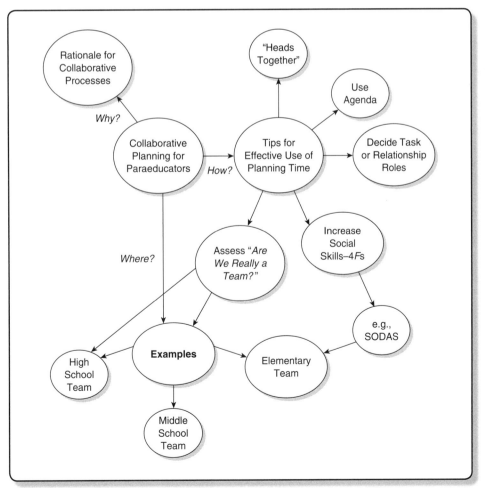

Figure 4.1
Concept Map for Collaborative Planning Processes for Paraeducators

Ask a paraeducator or the educators who work with them what allows them to be successful—among the top responses will be "collaborative planning." In this chapter, you will discover how paraeducators and classroom teachers conduct collaborative meetings. Figure 4.1 shows a concept map[2] interconnecting the ideas in this chapter. We hope you'll find new insights to the following questions.

- Why is the collaborative planning process so important?
- What are some strategies to make planning processes more efficient?
- What are some tips for developing interpersonal relationships among team members?
- How are effective planning teams assessed?

You will learn about advice and tips for efficient planning among school personnel and how Ms. Hernandez, Ms. Bartolo, and Mr. Anderson engage in collaborative planning with their teams.

■ WHY IS THE COLLABORATIVE PLANNING PROCESS SO IMPORTANT?

Collaborative planning makes it possible for planning team members to experience synergy (Hourcade & Bauwens, 2002). Others have described this as the "two heads are better than one" phenomenon (Thousand & Villa, 2000). Through collaborative planning, team members experience higher-level thinking and generate more novel solutions (Thousand, Villa, Nevin, & Paolucci-Whitcomb, 1995). The basic human needs proposed by Glasser (1999) of survival, power, freedom or choice, sense of belonging, and fun also can be met through the interactive interchanges that occur through the collaborative planning process. Each team member's chance for *survival* and *power* in educating diverse learners increases through the exchange or resources and expertise. Team members experience *belonging* and *freedom* from isolation as well as *fun*, as they jointly engage in stimulating dialogue and creative solution finding.

One way for team members to start the planning process is to interview one another to discover each person's strengths, preferences, and specialized skills. Many studies have been conducted to determine the importance of intrapersonal, interpersonal, and specialized skills (Idol, Nevin, & Paolucci-Whitcomb, 2000). Intrapersonal skills are those that involve knowing your feelings, values, and attitudes. Interpersonal skills such as communication, problem solving, and teamwork allow you to work with others harmoniously and efficiently. Specialized knowledge

---

2. Figure 4.1 is an example of a "spider" concept map where ideas are organized around the central theme or unifying factor. Outwardly radiating sub-themes surround the center. Concept maps are easy to use and can help many learners understand how complex ideas relate to each other. For information on four different categories of concept maps, see http://classes.aces.uiuc.edu/ACES100/Mind/c-m2.html.

and skills are unique to your own experiences and background (e.g., speaking a second or third language, knowing how to type or use a computer, differentiating instruction materials).

Resource D of this book offers a self-assessment tool entitled "Team Summary: Our Likes and Dislikes When Working With Others." This tool can be used to help new collaborative team members get to know each other's backgrounds by engaging in particular behaviors important to team success. The use of such a tool not only can increase teaching team members' awareness and respect for one another's strengths but can provide an ongoing method of encouraging teammates to add to their skill sets. You can see a completed summary for Ms. Bartolo's middle school team on p. 52.

STRATEGIES TO MAKE PLANNING PROCESSES MORE EFFICIENT ■

If collaborative planning is such a good practice, how do we get more time to plan during school hours? How do we do it well, so that the benefits are realized? What can be done to make collaborative planning more effective and efficient?

One resource in scarce supply in today's schools is time for planning, reflecting, or problem solving. While finding, creating, expanding, or rearranging time for planning is an enduring educational challenge, the real challenge becomes how to *effectively use* the time we do have. Often it is not how much time for planning finally is set aside but how *efficiently* team members do business when they actually sit down face-to-face.

Collaborative planning is best accomplished when people literally put their heads together, in face-to-face meetings. Planning meetings are more likely to be both effective *and* efficient when a structured meeting format is used, such as the Collaborative Planning Meeting Agenda (Thousand & Villa, 2000; Villa et al., 2008a) found as Resource E of this book. This meeting agenda format helps to make sure that team members practice four critical elements of an effective cooperative planning process: positive interdependence, group processing, social skills, and face-to-face interaction. On page 49, you can see a completed agenda for one of the Wednesday planning meetings held by Ms. Hernandez's second-grade team.

Positive interdependence is structured by distributing leadership among group members by assigning and rotating roles. Roles may be task-related (e.g., timekeeper or recorder) or relationship-oriented (e.g., encourager or praiser). Roles are assigned in advance of the next meeting. See Table 4.1 for sample roles. Assigning roles in advance ensures that each person has the materials needed to carry out his or her role (e.g., the timekeeper has a watch or timer, the recorder has chart paper and markers and/or a computer to record minutes). Assigning roles in advance also prompts coteachers to rotate roles and, in this way, creates a sense of distributed responsibility and positive interdependence. The meeting agenda format also prompts planning team members to be *positively interdependent* in completing actions by distributing among team members agreed-upon action items with due dates in the section of the agenda labeled "Outcomes."

Table 4.1
Task and Relationship
Roles for Planning
Meetings

Task Roles	
Timekeeper	The Timekeeper monitors the time, encourages planning team members to stop at agreed-upon times, and alerts members when the end of the agreed-upon time period is approaching. "We have five minutes left to finish."
Recorder	The Recorder writes down the decisions made by the team and distributes copies to all present and to absent members within one week's time.
Summarizer	The Summarizer summarizes outcomes of a discussion before moving on to a new topic.
Checker	The Checker makes sure members understand discussion and decisions. "Can you explain how we arrived at this decision?"
Relationship Roles	
Encourager	The Encourager encourages all team members to participate and carry out their roles.
Praiser	The Praiser lets team members know when they are using collaborative skills that positively impact each other. The Praiser is careful to make the praise sound and feel authentic as well as specific (e.g., "Thanks, Rich, for keeping us focused on our tasks!") rather than general (e.g., "Good job!").
Jargon Buster	The Jargon Buster lets team members know when they are using terms such as acronyms or abbreviations that someone might not understand (e.g., "Oops, does anyone not know what IEP means?").

The use of *social skills* is prompted and monitored by way of a pause in the agenda for *group processing* of how group members are treating one another and feeling about their task completion. This occurs both midway through and at the end of the meeting. *Face-to-face interaction* is prompted and recognized with the public recording of (a) who is present, (b) who is late, (c) who is absent from the meeting, and (d) the next meeting's agenda for continued face-to-face planning. Overall, using a planning system that encourages effective communication among team members, including paraeducators, helps everyone (a) build relationships and (b) realize how important they are to the success of the learners in their school. French (2007) suggests that, whenever possible, paraeducators take the opportunity to build relationships by engaging in other *face-to-face interaction* events such as birthday parties and baby showers for staff and faculty meetings and inservice training events.

■ TIPS FOR DEVELOPING INTERPERSONAL RELATIONSHIPS AMONG TEAM MEMBERS

An important first step in developing team member relationships is to devote time to learning about one another's cultural, personal, and professional backgrounds as well as each member's experiences with collaborative teaming (Webb-Johnson, 2002). It helps team members to know that working and planning with others is a process that goes through stages and requires team members to learn, practice, and use four sets of social skills: forming, functioning, formulating, and fermenting skills (Johnson & Johnson, 1997). Knowing about these skill sets can help teammates *choose to use* specific skills, as needed, to help the team accomplish goals and, at the same time, develop and maintain positive relationships.

When new teams first are *forming,* the goal is to build mutual and reciprocal trust. Trust-building behaviors include arriving on time and staying for the entire meeting, knowing and using teammates' names, and actively listening to one another. An important first agenda item for any new team is to discuss and agree upon common interpersonal ground rules or norms (e.g., waiting to interject a comment until after a teammate has finished speaking or using each person's preferred name). Norms are "a group's common beliefs regarding appropriate behavior for members; they tell, in other words, how members are expected to behave.... All groups have norms, set either formally or informally" (Johnson & Johnson, 1997, p. 424). By explicitly stating and committing to adhere to norms, team members create a sense of safety for each other to share information with one another and to risk to "tell the truth" about concerns and needs.

The stages of development of positive interpersonal relationships within a group—Forming, Functioning, Formulating, Fermenting—are shown in Table 4.2. As members develop trust in *forming* their team, they begin to pay attention to *functioning* skills that promote either goal achievement or continued development of positive interpersonal relationships. Functioning skills include clarifying one's own views, coordinating tasks, paraphrasing the views of others, and checking for understanding of and agreement with team decisions. *Formulating* skills are those creative problem-solving skills that help teams creatively solve expected and unexpected challenges.

Formulating skills include creative problem-solving skills such as brainstorming, seeking of additional information through questioning, and meta-cognition (i.e., thinking about and explaining out loud how you think and make decisions). Other skills related to the *formulating* stage include asking for critical feedback and taking risks to try out unfamiliar practices. The final set of teaming skills, *fermenting* skills, are those conflict resolution skills that allow you and your teammates to deal with the controversies and conflicts that are inevitable within every planning team. *Fermenting* skills become even more important when there are "high stakes" goals to achieve, such as when your team wants to ensure the academic, social, and emotional success of all students.

When collaborative planning team members can engage in and comfortably manage conflicting opinions and controversy, the team becomes more successful than those teams that avoid conflict. Skills involved in constructive controversy include criticizing ideas, not people; differentiating between various or conflicting opinions; asking for more information and underlying rationale in order to understand someone else's position; and using creative problem-solving techniques.

When you know and practice the skills related to the four *F*s of interpersonal relationships, you allow for the clashing of ideas because you know that this clash actually stimulates the integration of the ideas into

Forming Stage (Trust-Building) Skills
_____ Use teammates' preferred names.
_____ Use affirming statements (i.e., enforce a "no put-downs" norm).
_____ Come to meetings on time and stay for the entire time.
_____ Demonstrate trustworthiness by following through on agreements.
_____ Acknowledge teammates for their follow-through.
Functioning Stage (Communication and Leadership) Skills
_____ Clarify the team's tasks, goals, and responsibilities.
_____ Set or call attention to the time limits.
_____ Suggest procedures on how to perform a task effectively.
_____ Express support and acceptance verbally.
_____ Paraphrase and clarify.
_____ Energize the group with humor, ideas, and enthusiasm.
_____ Describe feelings, when appropriate.
Formulating Stage (Creative Solution-Finding) Skills
_____ Summarize what has been said.
_____ Seek accuracy by correcting or adding to the summary.
_____ Seek connections to other knowledge.
_____ Seek clever ways to remember ideas, facts, and decisions.
_____ Ask teammates to explain the reasoning behind their positions.
Fermenting Stage (Conflict Resolution) Skills
_____ Criticize ideas without criticizing people.
_____ Differentiate ideas where there is disagreement.
_____ Integrate different ideas into a single position.
_____ Probe by asking questions that lead to deeper understanding.
_____ Suggest new answers and ideas.
_____ Think of new ways to resolve differences of opinion.

new and novel solutions. Knowing these skills can push you and your teammates to a higher level of cohesiveness and a higher sense of owning the solutions. Together, you learn that your team can not only survive but also actually thrive as a result of working through the conflict.

Because both effectiveness and enjoyment increase when you and your team members understand and consciously practice interpersonal social skills, the list in Table 4.2 can be used to guide your reflective conversations about social skill use during *group processing* in the middle and at the end of your team meetings. We encourage teams to add to this list any other interpersonal skills their team members agree are important to develop and practice.

HOW EFFECTIVE PLANNING ■
TEAMS ARE ASSESSED

As emphasized in the previous paragraph, when planning team members are aware of the specific desired collaborative behaviors that help them to be productive, they are in the position to self-assess and set goals for improving their face-to-face planning experiences. A self-assessment tool entitled "Checklist: Are We Really a Collaborative Team?" (Resource F) includes 20 items that represent the four elements of an effective team (i.e., face-to-face interaction, positive interdependence, group processing, and social skills). Team members answer each item on the checklist using a Yes/No format. You will see in Figure 4.4 how one of Mr. Anderson's secondary school teams uses the checklist to diagnose its current status with regard to the four elements of effective teaming.

We suggest that you and your teammates periodically use this checklist both to celebrate your team's strengths and to prompt a conversation about elements that might need to be improved. A useful decision rule for giving an item a "Yes" rating is that *every* team member definitely agrees to the "Yes" rating. This reduces the temptation to pressure anyone with a differing perception to give up that perspective for the sake of consensus and, at the same time, encourages real dialogue about differing perceptions about the team planning experience.

MS. HERNANDEZ: ELEMENTARY SCHOOL ■
COLLABORATIVE PLANNING SCENARIO

On Wednesdays, the faculty at Chaparral Valley Elementary School (CVES) and all elementary schools in the district have a reduced teaching schedule when the children are released early (i.e., at noon rather than 2:30 p.m.) so that the faculty and staff can meet, plan, or engage in professional development. Each school within the district has discretion as to how this time may be used, but it is intended to be used for the purposes of improving student success through staff engaging in professional development, curriculum mapping, meeting as collaborative teams, and so forth. Historically, paraeducators were not paid or expected to stay for this time. However, as part of the service delivery re-design at CVES, the principal made it a priority to have Ms. Hernandez's contracted five hours on Wednesday include the first one and a quarter hours of Wednesday afternoons. This makes it possible for her to participate as a planning team member.

The school staff collectively agreed that the Block Reading Intervention Toward Excellence, or BRITE, differentiated literacy group time would not be scheduled on Wednesdays, because the time devoted to content instruction already was reduced to accommodate the early release. Instead, after students are dismissed at noon, grade-level teams meet from noon to 1 p.m. over lunch. Approximately half of that hour is dedicated to curriculum alignment and other grade-level issues. The remaining 30 or so minutes are devoted to decisions about the BRITE differentiated literacy time. During this 30-minute block of time, team members examine and monitor student data that was generated during the *differentiated literacy group time* instructional blocks. In this way, they can adjust instructional methods and assign students to new groups, based upon each student's progress. The second- and third-grade team members agreed that conversations about second grade's BRITE time would occur during the first 30 minutes, whereas conversations about third grade's BRITE time would occur during the last 30 minutes. This means Ms. Hernandez and the special education teacher who supports both teams can be present for conversations at both grade-level meetings.

Because the Wednesday team meetings are brief, team members need to be efficient in how they use their time together. As a consequence, Ms. Hernandez's teams adopt some strategies that Melony Helprin, the team's special educator, learned in her credential program about effective meetings. First, they build an agenda before the face-to-face meetings, using the agenda format included as Resource E. They also check their e-mails the day before to verify or add new items, such as problem solving for a student who might be in crisis for one reason or another.

Figure 4.2 shows a 35-minute agenda for Ms. Hernandez's second-grade collaborative planning sessions. The agenda indicates who was present, who was absent, and what the tasks to be accomplished were. The agenda shows the team assigned and rotated roles, including several of those discussed in Table 4.1. Third, the team made sure they saved a couple of minutes to process how effectively they had accomplished their agenda tasks, maintained their positive interpersonal relationships, and kept the lines of communication open. To Ms. Hernandez, at first it seems awkward and formal to have so much structure. However, she begins to appreciate the structure, because she realizes how much needs to be accomplished in such a short time and how wasteful it can be when team members' conversations are not focused on the task.

The team members really improved their efficiency when Melony taught them a simple and quick creative problem-solving format known as "having a SODAS" during a faculty inservice meeting last year. The acronym SODAS represents five steps in problem-solving: identifying the (a) Situation, (b) Options, (c) Disadvantages, (d) Advantages, and (e) Solution to a problem (Hazel, Schumaker, Sherman, & Sheldon, 1995). Using the SODAS template shown in Resource G, a team identifies a problem situation, brainstorms several solutions, identifies the disadvantages and advantages of each proposed solution, and settles upon a preferred solution to their problem. The faculty and paraeducators for the second- and third-grade teams often use SODAS as an objective way to develop lots of potential ideas and then to focus on one or two viable options. A plan of action is then settled upon and put into motion.

Ms. Hernandez notices that the SODAS strategy is used with the second- and third-grade students, all of whom had been taught how to use the process to resolve their own problems. All of the second- and third-grade teachers have a stack of SODAS forms on their desk under a soda can. When students describe problems or issues with classmates, the teachers first encourage the students to "have SODAS" and talk it out among themselves using the SODAS procedures.

Another collaborative teaming strategy at CVES is to bring the entire staff together once a month for shared inservice events and conversations. On these designated Wednesday afternoons, meetings are complemented

People present: Robin, Suyapa, Tim, Sidia, Carlotta, Melony	Absentees: Wanda, Literacy (conducting district training)	Others who need to know: Suzanne Schmidt, Principal
Roles Timekeeper Recorder Checker	**This meeting** Melony Helprin Sidia Sooze Carlotta Hernandez	**Next meeting** Tim Drumming Robin Dahl Suyapa Prada

Agenda

Agenda Items	Time limit
1. Review agenda and positive comments	2 minutes
2. Examine student data for past 2 weeks	10 minutes
3. Make decisions on groupings for next 2 weeks	10 minutes
4. Pause for group processing of progress toward task accomplishment and use of interpersonal skills	1 minute
5. Problem solve for individual student challenges	5 minutes
6. Other: To be determined	5 minutes
7. Final group processing of task and relationship	2 minutes

Minutes of Outcomes

Action Items	Person(s) Responsible	By When?
1. Communicate outcomes to absent members and others	Sidia (recorder) e-mails minutes to everyone	2 p.m. today
2. Prepare materials	Everyone	Tomorrow

Agenda Building for Next Meeting

Date: Wed., December 3rd	Time: Noon	Location: Tim's Classroom

Expected agenda items
   1. Semester summative assessment schedule 2. Data analysis and January regroupings 3. Individual student concerns

Figure 4.2
Agenda for Ms. Hernandez's Second-Grade Collaborative Team Planning Session

with a *lunch and learn* event where grade-level teams rotate responsibility for providing lunch for everyone. At this time, the faculty and staff participate in professional development activities related to literacy instruction. The content of this *lunch and learn* experience is usually identified by the literacy core team (i.e., the principal, the reading specialist, the special educator, and the district literacy consultant). However, anyone can take the lead to share a new strategy or learning outcome. In fact, it was at one of the early *lunch and learns* in the previous year that Melony, Ms. Hernandez's special education supervisor, introduced the SODAS problem-solving format that many of the teachers adopted as a quick way to turn problems back to the students. Ms. Hernandez thinks about teaching SODAS to her own two children, so they can resolve their own conflicts. She also finds herself wondering whether paraeducators ever take the lead to teach something at the *lunch and learn* events.

Ms. Hernandez appreciates that she is compensated through 1:15 p.m. so she can benefit from all of the Wednesday meetings. And she especially enjoys the sense of community that occurs during lunch and learn events on Wednesdays. She encourages all of her part-time paraeducator colleagues to stay for the free lunch and informal and fun learning opportunity, and most do, even though they are not paid to stay past noon. By the fourth week of the new school year, Ms. Hernandez realizes that, in addition to affecting students, the change to a team approach to supporting all students improves her own satisfaction as a paraeducator. Many pieces to the collaborative planning and teaming process puzzle come together for her and the students. For example, she notices that the boys who had been such a problem for her to handle the previous year in the resource room now seem more motivated to stay focused and in control of their behavior so they can remain in the general education classroom whether during *differentiated literacy group time* or the rest of the day. She also notices how much more satisfied she is when she is teaching students with and without disabilities in the general education classroom rather than staying in the resource room all day long. Her job is much more fun, less isolating, and less fragmented. She becomes more confident in her teaching because she receives ongoing modeling, training, and feedback from the reading specialist as well as the special educator on specific literacy interventions. Plus, she now has access to the literacy development resources brought in by the literacy specialist. Prior to the merging of programs and students this year, she and her supervising special education teacher never had access to these materials.

At the weekly Wednesday collaborative planning meetings, Ms. Hernandez observes firsthand how much her second- and third-grade teammates begin to genuinely care about *all* of the students in each of the grades. She hears them talking about *their* students rather than the "English learners" or "special education" or "regular" students. Ms. Hernandez develops a healthy appreciation for regular assessments; the daily and weekly data collected on student performance really show everyone what is and what is not working. She thinks the best part of the job is when her teams make adjustments right away. This means students can move into new groupings, work with different teachers, learn from materials, and experience instructional methods that might be more effective for their learning styles.

■ MS. BARTOLO: MIDDLE SCHOOL COLLABORATIVE PLANNING SCENARIO

Both English teachers, Ms. Hendrickson and Ms. Cole, share a planning and lunch period with Ms. Bartolo. From the start of the school year, both teachers committed to meeting for 30 minutes once a week with Ms. Bartolo. As a result of these planned meetings and the informal planning that occurs during the shared lunch period, Ms. Bartolo begins to feel more capable and competent in her role as a paraeducator in both of the English classes.

Ms. Bartolo follows advice from the two English teachers to develop her own job description. With the help of Ms. Hendrickson and Ms. Cole, she analyzes the Co-Teaching Roles and Responsibilities Matrix (see Resource A and Table 3.5) for her team and develops a draft job description to review with her supervising special educator, Ms. Brinkley. The meeting with Ms. Brinkley goes extremely well. Ms. Bartolo feels validated that the co-teaching roles she practiced in the English classes as well as in the science class were what was expected of her. Ms. Brinkley promises to edit the job description and bring it to a meeting with all of the teachers with whom Ms. Bartolo works. The purpose of the meeting is not only to finalize a job description but to clarify for all of the general educators Ms. Bartolo's duties and responsibilities in their classrooms.

After discussing the job description, Ms. Bartolo shares her concerns about her role with Bradley (the student with autism) and her role in Mr. Ruhan's science class. Ms. Brinkley agrees that it is important for Ms. Bartolo to have some modeling of how to work with Bradley and makes a date to work with Bradley in the learning center at the end of the following week. They also discuss setting up weekly meetings so Ms. Brinkley can provide Ms. Bartolo with clinical supervision. Ms. Bartolo requests that these meetings be held during the period when she provides clerical duties in the special education director's office, so that she will not lose time with students. Ms. Brinkley agrees that this would be a great time to meet but is unable to do so as she is co-teaching at that time in a geometry class. Ms. Brinkley asks whether Ms. Bartolo can meet after school one day a week. Ms. Bartolo agrees. Even though Ms. Bartolo will not receive monetary compensation for the additional time required for the meeting, Ms. Brinkley can grant her compensatory time so that she can leave 30 or 40 minutes early on Fridays.

Before the meeting ends, Ms. Bartolo tells Ms. Brinkley about her failed efforts to meet the science teacher, Mr. Ruhan, after school to clarify her role. Every time she has asked him to meet he has stated that he is too busy to do so. Because Mr. Ruhan is a new teacher, Ms. Brinkley advises Ms. Bartolo to give Mr. Ruhan a couple more weeks to adjust to the school and the students. She again promises Ms. Bartolo she will schedule the meeting to discuss the job description with Ms. Cole, Ms. Hendrickson, and Mr. Ruhan within three weeks and will be sure Mr. Ruhan is clear as to Ms. Bartolo's role in his classroom by the time the meeting is over.

Ms. Brinkley is sensitive to the possibility that Mr. Ruhan might feel defensive and "ganged up on" when Ms. Bartolo's role is clarified in the upcoming meeting, so she wants to begin the meeting with some type of "getting to know you" activity before pushing for changes in Ms. Bartolo's role and responsibilities in his classroom. She has used the "Our Likes and Dislikes When Working With Others" team summary (see Resource D) to help newly formed teams become familiar with their members' strengths and likes and dislikes about certain roles in meetings. So, she plans to start the upcoming meeting by having everyone complete the form.

Three weeks later, at the meeting, the team completes the "Our Likes and Dislikes When Working With Others" team summary. Figure 4.3 shows how each person rated himself or herself on the teaming behaviors

Figure 4.3
Ms. Bartolo's Team's Completed "Our Likes and Dislikes When Working With Others" Team Summary

Directions: Indicate which items you enjoy doing when working with others on a team. When all team members have indicated their preferences, discuss your team's summary profile. What are the strengths of team members? Given these preferences and skills, what issues or challenges should be easy or exciting for your team to address? What kinds of problems might you anticipate among team members?

Collaborative Behaviors During and Following Meetings	Brinkley	Ruhan	Cole	Hendrickson	Bartolo
Serving as a Recorder			X		
Serving as a Timekeeper	X	X			
Sharing information	X		X	X	X
Asking for help	X		X	X	
Asking questions			X	X	X
Encouraging participation	X		X		
Being a Process Observer	X				
Sharing feelings				X	X
Dealing with conflict	X				
Assuming leadership	X		X	X	
Following an agenda	X	X	X		
Analyzing problems		X			
Accepting criticism of my ideas	X			X	
Weighing pros and cons of options before making decisions	X				
Brainstorming	X	X	X	X	
Listening to people describe their feelings			X		X
Compromising			X	X	X
Summarizing		X			
Delegating tasks to someone else	X		X	X	
Changing the way I do things					X
Being diplomatic	X				
Speaking	X		X	X	
Listening		X			
Goal setting	X	X		X	

Collaborative Behaviors During and Following Meetings	Brinkley	Ruhan	Cole	Hendrickson	Bartolo
Meeting deadlines		X			
Giving others recognition and credit	X		X		
Doing research		X			
Data collection		X			
Other: _____					

ACTION PLAN:

How will you deal proactively with future conflicts or disagreements?

_____

_____

What training opportunities might team members arrange or take advantage of to increase your team members' collaborative skills?

_____

_____

Are there any other individuals with complementary skills that you might want to add to your team?

_____

_____

listed in the summary. Everyone commented that it was both illuminating and fun to compare the similarities and differences among themselves among these collaborative behaviors. After completing the checklist, everyone agrees to think about how they might answer discussion question prompts included the summary's directions. These questions include the following:

- What are the strengths of team members?
- Given these preferences and skills, what issue or challenges should be easy or exciting for your team to address?
- What kinds of problems might you anticipate among team members?

They agree to meet again the following week at the same time and in the same location. Ms. Brinkley distributes Ms. Bartolo's job description, which she has slightly modified from the draft Ms. Bartolo crafted. Ms. Brinkley asks the team members to take some time between now and next week's meeting to examine the elements of the job description and come up with any questions of clarification they might discuss and resolve so that the job description can be finalized.

■ MR. ANDERSON: SECONDARY SCHOOL COLLABORATIVE PLANNING SCENARIO

Mr. Anderson has been impressed with the weekly instructional planning meetings that he attends with Ms. Bennevento, the social studies teacher; Mr. Schwab, the science teacher; and Ms. Clooney, the special educator. He feels that their meetings are so well organized that they are able to accomplish many tasks and, at the same time, have fun at their meetings. At these meetings, Ms. Clooney shares several tools and strategies for facilitating team meetings she learned about in courses she took in her credential program.

One such tool, the "Are We Really a Collaborative Team?" checklist (Resource F), is specifically designed to have teams examine the four elements of an effective collaborative team (i.e., positive interdependence, social skills, group processing, and face-to-face interaction). The team agrees that after one month of working together, each team member will independently complete the "Are We Really a Collaborative Team?" checklist and subsequently compare their responses. Figure 4.4 shows the results of the four team members' first self-assessment using this checklist. Because there are 20 items and four team members, a maximum total score in either column (i.e., "yes" or "no") would be 80. They celebrate when they discover they have almost universal agreement on their individual responses to the checklist (i.e., collectively 56 "yes" versus 22 "no" responses).

They discuss the checklist items on which they do not agree and those for which they answered "no" instead of "yes." The team sets goals for addressing several of the items, especially (a) starting and ending on time and (b) updating tardy members at a break or after the meeting rather than during the meeting. They promise to re-administer the checklist in three months and once again six weeks prior to the end of the school year. They believe that this regular self-assessment process will keep them motivated to use the strategies that fostered effective collaborative teaming.

■ SUMMARY

You may feel that this chapter is jam-packed with new ideas for you to use as you collaboratively plan with others on the team to provide the best learning environments for students. We hope you are now able to create your own answers to the guiding questions posed at the beginning of the chapter. For example, do the elements of collaborative planning ring true

Directions: For a team score, mark a check under Yes or No for each of the 20 statements.

Figure 4.4
Mr. Anderson's Team's Completed "Are We Really a Collaborative Team?" Checklist

Yes	No	In our collaborative planning meetings:
		Face-to-Face Interactions
4		1. Do we meet in a comfortable environment?
3	1	2. Do we arrange ourselves in a circle so we can hear each other and see each other's facial expressions?
4		3. Is our group size manageable (6 or fewer members)?
3	1	4. Do we meet regularly at times and locations agreed upon in advance by teammates?
4		5. Do we use a structured agenda with time limits for agenda items agreed upon at the previous meeting?
4		6. Do needed members receive a timely invitation? (Note: Needed members may change from meeting to meeting, based upon agenda items.)
2	2	7. Do we start and end on time?
	4	8. Do we update tardy members at a break or after the meeting rather than stopping the meeting midstream?
		Positive Interdependence
4		9. Have we publicly discussed and agreed upon the group's overall goals, purposes, and responsibilities?
4		10. Do we distribute leadership by rotating roles (e.g., recorder, timekeeper, encourager, agreement checker)?
4		11. Do we start each meeting with positive comments and devote time to celebrating successes?
1	3	12. Do we have fun at our meetings?
		Social Skills
4		13. Have we established a set of group ground rules or norms and committed to abiding by these norms?
4		14. Do we explain the group's norms to new members?
4		15. Do we create an atmosphere for safely expressing genuine perspectives (negative and positive)?
2	2	16. Do we acknowledge and deal with conflict during meetings?
1	3	17. Do we have a communication system for absent members and people who are not regular team members but who need to know about our decisions (e.g., administrators)?
2	2	18. Do we agree on the process for making a particular decision (e.g., majority vote, consensus, unanimous decision)?
		Group Processing
2	2	19. Do we build in time at the end of each meeting to reflect upon and set goals for improving our interactions during meetings?
2	2	20. Do we study about or arrange for training to improve targeted social skills (e.g., conflict resolution or mediation)?
58	**22**	**TOTAL (Out of maximum of 20 items × number of team members)** **(Out of 80 total points in each column)**

with your own experiences? Can you imagine yourself as a contributing member of a planning team? Do you now have strategies to use to make planning processes more efficient?

We wonder to what extent you agree with the tips and advice for developing positive interrelationships with members of your team. Perhaps some of the tips that we suggest are counter to what you know is true, especially if you are a member of a culturally or linguistically diverse group. It's important to know what is effective for you!

Do you now have some tools to assess your effectiveness as a member of a teaching team? What methods might you suggest in addition to the ones we offer? Remember that one of the best ways to improve team effectiveness is to make it possible for others to understand what you, personally, want to improve! So please be willing to (a) share your goals and (b) support others as they share what they want to improve.

In the next chapter, you will discover ways to implement collaborative teaching approaches.

5

Co-Teaching and Collaborative Teaching Approaches

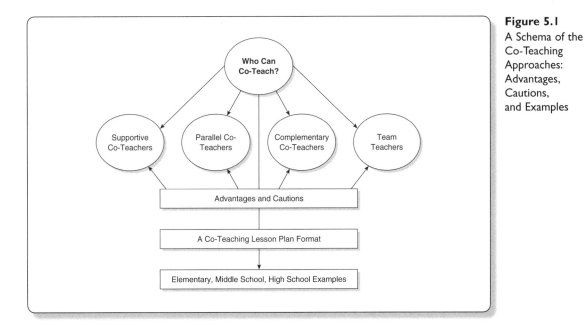

Figure 5.1
A Schema of the Co-Teaching Approaches: Advantages, Cautions, and Examples

As Figure 5.1 indicates, in this chapter you will learn the answers to several questions about collaborative teaching approaches in today's classrooms:

- Who can be a co-teacher?

- What are the four approaches to co-teaching that paraeducators are most likely to experience when they help students in the general education classroom?
- How can paraeducators be co-teachers?
- In what ways does a co-teaching lesson plan format help to guide instruction?

WHO CAN BE A CO-TEACHER?

First, we'll discuss our (the authors') experiences related to the question, "Who can be a co-teacher?" We have found that *anyone who has an instructional role* in a school can co-teach. Co-teaching is not just for credentialed or certificated personnel (i.e., classroom teachers, special and bilingual educators, content specialists such as reading teachers, and support personnel such as speech and language therapists and school psychologists). Co-teaching roles can be effectively carried out by paraeducators, volunteers, and students themselves. In fact, children and youths who learn and practice being student co-teachers—whether that means co-teaching with an adult, peer tutoring, cooperative group learning, dialogue teaching, or instructional conversation—are more likely to increase their retention and achievement with academic content but also grow into adults who are more effective advocates for themselves (for more details see Villa et al., 2008a).

In a comprehensive national survey, educators experienced in meeting the needs of students in a diverse classroom reported that they used four predominant co-teaching approaches—supportive co-teaching, parallel co-teaching, complementary co-teaching, and team teaching—to collaborate instructionally (National Center on Educational Restructuring and Inclusion, 1995). Before describing each approach, it is important to emphasize that none of these four co-teaching approaches is better than another. In all of the approaches to co-teaching, the overarching goal is to gather additional human resources to support student learning (Villa et al., 2008a, 2008c). Many teachers who are new to having others work with them in a classroom begin with supportive co-teaching because this approach can involve less planning and structured coordination among co-teaching team members. As co-teaching skills and relationships strengthen, co-teachers then often venture into the parallel, complementary, and team co-teaching approaches that require more time, coordination, and knowledge of and trust in one another's skills.

THE FOUR APPROACHES TO CO-TEACHING THAT PARAEDUCATORS ARE MOST LIKELY TO EXPERIENCE WHEN THEY HELP STUDENTS IN THE GENERAL EDUCATION CLASSROOM

Supportive Co-Teaching

Supportive co-teaching is when one co-teacher takes the lead instructional role and the other rotates among the students to provide support.

The co-teacher taking the supportive role watches or listens as students work together, stepping in to provide one-to-one tutorial assistance when necessary, while the other co-teacher continues to direct the lesson. The supportive co-teacher may provide academic, behavioral, or communication support to students in the classroom, and there may be more than one supportive co-teacher.

An advantage of supportive co-teaching, when done correctly, is that the ratio of adults to students is increased as both teachers have shared responsibility for all the students in the classroom. Students often appreciate having the extra help that two or more co-teachers in the classroom can offer.

A caution when using the supportive teaching approach is that whoever is playing the support role (e.g., special educator or bilingual translator) must not become "Velcroed" to individual students, functioning as hovercraft vehicles blocking students' interactions with other students. This can be stigmatizing for both students and the support person, leading students to perceive that the student and support teacher are not genuine members of the classroom. Also beware of not using to the best advantage the skills of another educator locked into the supportive role.

Parallel Co-Teaching

Parallel co-teaching is when two or more people work with different groups of students in different sections of the classroom. In this setup, both (or all) co-teachers have shared responsibility for all the students in the classroom. As shown in Table 5.1, parallel co-teaching can have seven variations: split class, station teaching or learning centers, co-teachers rotate, each co-teacher cooperative group monitoring, experiment or lab monitoring, learning style focus, or supplementary instruction.

A major advantage of the parallel co-teaching approach is that students can experience multiple options for how to access the learning material. This means that their particular learning preferences, learning styles, and learning needs are more likely to be met.

Two cautions are important to recognize when parallel teaching. Primarily, there is the possibility of creating a special class within a class by routinely assigning the same students in the same group with the same co-teacher. It is important, therefore, to allow students to learn with others with different ways of approaching learning by deliberately keeping groups heterogeneous, whenever possible. It also is important to rotate students among different co-teachers so students may stretch their learning by experiencing different instructors' approaches and expertise. This can avoid stigmatization that may arise if someone other than the classroom teacher (e.g., special educator) always teaches one set of students. Plus, if all members of the co-teaching team are familiar with all students, they are better able to problem solve any barriers to academic, communication, and social learning that their common students encounter. Beware of the negative impact on assessment measures when students of low ability are primarily grouped with other students of low ability (Marzano, Pickering, & Pollack, 2001, p. 87).

Split Class	Each co-teacher is responsible for a particular group of students, monitoring understanding and providing guided instruction including re-teaching the group, if necessary.
Station Teaching or Learning Centers	Each co-teacher is responsible for assembling, guiding, and monitoring one or more learning centers or stations.
Co-Teachers Rotate	The co-teachers rotate among two or more groups of students, with each co-teacher teaching a different component of the lesson. This is similar to station teaching or learning centers, except that in this case the teachers rotate from group to group rather than having groups of students rotate from station to station.
Cooperative Group Monitoring	Each co-teacher takes responsibility for monitoring and providing feedback and assistance to a given number of cooperative groups of students.
Experiment or Lab Monitoring	Each co-teacher monitors and assists a given number of laboratory groups, providing guided instruction to groups that require additional support.
Learning Style Focus	One co-teacher works with a group of students using primarily visual strategies, another co-teacher works with a group using primarily auditory strategies, and yet another may work with a group using kinesthetic strategies.
Supplementary Instruction	One co-teacher works with the rest of the class on a concept or assignment, skill, or learning strategy. The other co-teacher (a) provides extra guidance on the concept or assignment to students who are self-identified or teacher-identified as needing extra assistance, (b) instructs students to apply or generalize the skill to a relevant community environment, (c) provides a targeted group of students with guided practice in how to apply the learning strategy to the content being addressed, or (d) provides enrichment activities.

Complementary Co-Teaching

Complementary co-teaching is when teaching team members do something to enhance the instruction provided by each other as they share responsibility for all the students in the classroom. For example, one classroom co-teacher might provide a lecture on the content while another co-teacher paraphrases statements and models note-taking on chart paper or a transparency.

One advantage of the complementary approach is that each partner can contribute to the quality of instruction by using and sharing his or her unique talents and areas of expertise. As this expertise is used and modeled, other members of the team have the opportunity to learn new techniques, methodologies, or procedures that they, in turn, can incorporate into their own teaching repertoire.

Because complementary co-teachers are jointly teaching and are often at the front of the room, it is critical to beware of too much teacher talk, too much repetition, and not enough structuring and monitoring of student–student interaction. A concern with complementary teaching, particularly at the secondary level, is that those who are not the content area experts may not have the same level of content mastery as the content teacher. This is unavoidable—and is not necessarily a drawback. Complementary teaching partners have expertise in other areas (e.g., speech and language pathologists have expertise in communication, a special educator has expertise in adapting curriculum and learning strategies, a paraeducator may speak fluent Spanish or another language that is the primary language for some of the students in the classroom, one member may be skilled in creating graphics that visually assist students to grasp new concepts or relationships between concepts) that can be readily used to complement and supplement the expertise of the content area teacher. Through planning and teaching together, all members of the team have an opportunity to acquire new skills. For example, the special educator may learn new content and the classroom teacher may acquire skills to differentiate curriculum, instruction, and assessment.

Team Teaching

Team teaching is when two or more people do what the traditional teacher has always done—plan, teach, assess, and assume responsibility for all of the students in the classroom. Team teachers have shared responsibility for all of the students in the classroom. They make decisions as to who does what before, during, and after the lesson so that there is equitable division of labor in planning and delivering lessons as well as in evaluating student progress. An advantage of the team teaching approach to co-teaching is that the co-teachers make decisions about which of the four co-teaching approaches they will use in a lesson based upon the content demands and the students' needs rather than the type of co-teaching approach they prefer or are most comfortable using. Frequently, co-teachers at this stage feel comfortable moving in and out of the various approaches within a lesson in response to student or task demands. The bottom line and test of a successful team teaching partnership is that all of the students view each person as "their teacher."

Advantages of the team teaching approach are similar to those for complementary co-teaching. Each team member can contribute to a lesson based upon his or her strengths. For example, for a lesson on inventions in science, one person whose interest is history could explain the impact on society. Another, whose strengths are more focused on the mechanisms involved, could explain how the particular inventions work. One person's interests and strengths might be in understanding and connecting students to how the culture itself uses the invention. In team teaching, every team member alternately leads, supports, and complements one another's instruction.

Team teachers need to heed the same cautions as those described for complementary co-teaching. Additionally, they need to recognize the natural human tendency to stay within our comfort zones. There is comfort in holding on to familiar and traditional roles (e.g., the history teacher providing the lecture and the special educator preparing and explaining the use of the lecture guide). To move from complementary to team teaching, partners have to trust one another to release to others their expertise and roles. This phenomenon of releasing one's knowledge, skills, and roles to another is known as *role release*. It is one of the hallmarks of a genuine and effective team teaching relationship.

■ HOW PARAEDUCATORS CAN BE CO-TEACHERS

A frequently asked question about paraeducators in the role of co-teachers is whether or not they can or should engage in all of the four co-teaching roles. To approach this question, take a moment to recall Ms. Hernandez, Ms. Bartolo, and Mr. Anderson. As we have tracked these paraeducators and their team members, you have learned a little about how each paraeducator on the teams has served in various co-teaching roles.

For all four co-teaching approaches, it is *possible* for paraeducators to provide meaningful instruction. Our experience has been that if paraeducators are to engage in complementary or team teaching co-teaching roles, at the very least there must be time for planning, and paraeducators need to have the benefit of careful training and supervision. Issues of paraeducator training and supervision for co-teaching are critical ones, frequently discussed in the literature (Ashbaker & Morgan, 2005; French, 2002; Gerlach, 2006; Picket & Gerlach, 2003) and are further explored in Chapter 6.

■ HOW A CO-TEACHING LESSON PLAN FORMAT HELPS TO GUIDE INSTRUCTION

As you learned in Chapter 3, paraeducators can be asked to support teachers at any point during the instructional process represented in Figure 3.2. Namely, for any given lesson or unit, a paraeducator may be invited to gather information about students in a class, participate in planning a lesson, carry out elements of a lesson, monitor student performance during the lesson and collect data on particular students, or reflect on and evaluate the effectiveness of the lesson.

Lesson plans allow paraeducators to understand what is expected of them during a lesson, grasp the big picture of the lesson, and understand the expectations of the students in the class. All of these pieces of information are offered in a carefully constructed lesson plan. Lesson plans increase the likelihood that a paraeducator, as well as the other co-teachers in the classroom, will differentiate and execute his or her responsibilities, be clear on expected student outcomes, note any needed adjustments for particular students, and ensure co-teacher communication. Paraeducators can and do provide valuable insights in developing lessons. However, remember that it is a legal requirement and the professional responsibility of credentialed and certified educators, rather than paraeducators, to take the lead in planning instruction and developing lesson plans for students.

We suggest the co-teaching lesson plan format in Resource H of this book for teachers to use when designing lessons and units in which they are co-teaching with paraeducators as well as other personnel. The lesson plan template, derived from our book *A Guide to Co-Teaching: Practical Tips for Facilitating Student Learning* (Villa et al., 2008a), asks co-teachers to think about the essential elements of any good lesson plan. It asks them to consider content dimensions—the lesson's objectives, the curriculum standard(s) addressed in the lesson, the materials needed by each partner, how student learning will be assessed, and any supplemental supports, aids, or services that might be needed for particular students. Because two or more co-teachers design this lesson plan for use, three additional questions remind co-teachers to deliberately consider the following:

1. Which of the four types of co-teaching arrangements will the team be using?

2. What exactly will each individual co-teacher be doing before, during, and after the lesson?

3. How will the room be arranged so that each co-teacher has the needed space to deliver instruction—and will instruction be delivered by one or more co-teachers in another space outside of the classroom, such as a learning center or the school library, for all or part of the lesson?

Collaboratively deciding how to answer these three questions ensures that co-teaching partners are clear about their own and each other's instructional roles and responsibilities. The final question in the co-teaching lesson plan asks where, when, and how co-teachers will debrief and evaluate the outcomes of the lesson. These questions ask co-teachers to reflect and engage in a recursive planning-analysis-reflection cycle that promotes co-teachers' communication and overall improvement in the quality of instruction.

In the next section, you will learn more about how Ms. Hernandez, Ms. Bartolo, and Mr. Anderson and their teachers co-teach. Can you detect which of the co-teaching approaches they are using and what are their roles and responsibilities related to the instructional cycle?

MS. HERNANDEZ: ELEMENTARY SCHOOL TEAM CO-TEACHING AND COLLABORATIVE APPROACHES

Parallel Co-Teaching During Second- and Third-Grade BRITE Differentiated Literacy Group Times

Ms. Hernandez and her second- and third-grade BRITE team members are a good example of educators using the parallel co-teaching approach to provide differentiated instruction in literacy. The two grade-level teams have strategically grouped students based upon what ongoing assessments suggest each student needs. The grade-level teams also discussed strengths-based information so as to balance their focus on students' challenges that an intervention approach such as RtI might seem to do. The team members know that tapping into student strengths, interests, and learning preferences is a key to student motivation, establishing a relationship, and determining what additional supports a student might need.

As we learned in previous chapters, the adults on each of Ms. Hernandez's grade-level teams meet every Wednesday at lunchtime to discuss student progress and to consider groupings and regroupings of students across each grade level's three classrooms for each grade level's BRITE differentiated literacy group time. Support personnel, including Ms. Hernandez, are distributed across classrooms during the BRITE literacy blocks. As Table 5.2 and Table 5.3 illustrate, in second and third grades, two of the three classrooms at each grade level include support personnel as co-teachers. In these two classrooms, the adults in the room generally engage in *parallel* co-teaching, where each adult focuses upon targeted specialized skills with a subset of the students who are in the room at the time.

The carefully planned schedule has three advantages. First, two or more adults are teaching in the *parallel* co-teaching structure in each classroom. Second, each of the seven members of the grade-level team collectively engages in parallel co-teaching across all three classrooms. Third, students may rotate among the *parallel* co-teaching groups within the class or across the classrooms. If students move to another group during the *differentiated literacy group time,* the students rather than the adults move between the classrooms.

Supportive, Parallel, and Complementary Co-Teaching in Second-Grade Homeroom Language Arts Time

When Ms. Hernandez moves from the BRITE *differentiated literacy group time* to join Suyapa Prada's dual immersion second-grade classroom for the hour of *homeroom language arts time*, she expands her co-teaching role to include supportive and complementary co-teaching. For example,

Table 5.2
Second-Grade BRITE Differentiated Literacy Group Time

Time Period	Ms. Robin Dahl, Classroom Teacher	Ms. Suyapa Prada, Dual Immersion Teacher	Mr. Tim Drumming, Classroom Teacher
8:15–9:15 a.m. (60 minutes)	Population: Students with least need for support in reading instruction (20–25 students)	Population: Students with some need for additional support in reading instruction (15–20 students, 2 educators, 5–10 students per group) Additional Support: Reading Specialist (Ms. Wanda Waldrich)	Population: Students in great need of support in reading instruction (25–30 students, 3 educators, 3–8 students per educator with smaller groups for students with most intensive needs) Additional Support: Special Educator (Ms. Melony Helprin) Speech and Language Specialist (Ms. Sidia Sooze) Paraeducator (Ms. Carlotta Hernandez)

Time Period	Ms. Rhonda Hart, Classroom Teacher	Mr. Tao Thom, Dual Immersion Classroom Teacher	Ms. Ginny Short, Classroom Teacher
9:20–10:20 a.m. (60 minutes)	Population: Students with least need for support in reading instruction (20–25 students)	Population: Students with some need for additional support in reading instruction (15–20 students, 2 educators, 5–10 students per group) Additional Support: Paraeducator (Ms. Carlotta Hernandez)	Population: Students in great need of support in reading instruction (25–30 students, 3 educators, 3–8 students per educator with smaller groups for students with most intensive needs) Additional Support: Special Educator (Ms. Melony Helprin) Reading Specialist (Ms. Wanda Waldrich) Literacy Tutor (Ms. Brenda Richards) Paraeducator (Ms. Carlotta Hernandez)

Table 5.3
Third-Grade BRITE Differentiated Literacy Group Time

Ms. Prada typically begins the *homeroom language arts time* with a whole class activity in which she reads a popular children's literature book selected by the children. During this time, Ms. Hernandez is in the *supportive* co-teaching role; she moves around the room to make sure all of the students have their books open and are following along.

Later in the *homeroom language arts time*, Ms. Prada sends students to four or five writing stations where they have differentiated options for composition assignments. One station features a speech-to-text program to assist in composing. At another station, students use word processing software and apply various editing functions such as spell check to their composition assignment(s). At yet other stations, students can examine and write about artifacts representing items featured in the story Ms. Prada read aloud. Here Ms. Hernandez typically is functioning in a *parallel* co-teaching role, as she is "in charge" of one or two of the stations while Ms. Prada manages the other stations. Ms. Prada e-mails Ms. Hernandez the instructions for her assigned station in time for Ms. Hernandez to review it, ask questions, and come prepared to work with students.

Sometimes, Ms. Prada asks Ms. Hernandez to model written expressions in both English and Spanish. The students have a graphic organizer and follow along as Ms. Prada teaches them how to use it. Ms. Hernandez writes the exact words used by the students on the graphic organizer, which is projected on the wall with a document projector. Ms. Hernandez has been told that what she is doing is known as *complementary* co-teaching.

Ms. Hernandez likes this term because she realizes she is indeed complementing the teacher's verbal instructions with a visual graphic organizer and also complementing the spoken language when she writes both English and Spanish equivalents.

Supportive, Parallel, and Complementary Co-Teaching in Third-Grade Homeroom Math Time

In Tao Thom's hour of *homeroom math time,* Ms. Hernandez's co-teaching roles are somewhat similar to her roles in Ms. Prada's class. Ms. Hernandez finds Mr. Thom's teaching style to be the most energetic she can imagine. She says, "Math class is like being in a whirlwind." Ms. Hernandez has been concerned about the boys with behavior support plans she taught in pullout math groups last year in the resource room who are now learning math in Mr. Thom's third-grade classroom. She remembers how difficult it once was for her to get them to focus on their math. However, in Mr. Thom's class, they seem to study their math like model students.

When Ms. Hernandez asks Mr. Thom why these boys are doing so well, he explains to her a little about the theory of multiple intelligences that he learned in his teacher-credentialing program (Armstrong, 2000; Gardner, 1999). He says he has noticed that there are several students, including these boys, who need to be active, who like changes in activities, and who appreciate music and movement while they learn. Consequently, each day, Mr. Thom begins math instruction with a song, a poem, a story, a theatrical demonstration, or a joke that includes math language. Mr. Thom tells Ms. Hernandez that this is how lessons began when he was a child in Vietnam. He is convinced that this technique energizes the students who have musical, rhythmic, verbal/linguistic, and kinesthetic intelligences and helps them view mathematics as a fun subject. Mr. Thom asks Ms. Hernandez to contribute her own poem, song, story, jingle, or joke.

Another daily feature of Mr. Thom's math period is the *math brain gym,* which is designed to tap into students' intelligences and provide physical exercise. During *math brain gym,* students stand and engage in physical exercises while reciting math facts, math vocabulary, or calling back answers to math brain teasers. Mr. Thom has Ms. Hernandez lead some of the brain gym exercises. He tells her he expects her to contribute to both the opening and brain gym exercises because he is convinced that all the students will respond better if they view her as an equal. Mr. Thom tells her that she is a *complementary* co-teacher with him. She enjoys sharing her songs and math exercises, even though she knows that Mr. Thom clearly is the content expert and she complements his teaching.

Like Ms. Prada, Mr. Thom differentiates instruction through the use of *parallel* co-teaching stations or learning centers that provide a wide variety of learning experiences. During station time, Mr. Thom monitors two groups as they travel from station to station while Ms. Hernandez monitors the other two groups. Mr. Thom and Ms. Hernandez switch the groups that they monitor from day to day, so that all students experience both co-teachers as their backup coach over the course of the week. Ms. Hernandez enjoys this *parallel* co-teaching structure, because she can observe the same students over the course of a single math period. This makes it easier for her to report any concerns about particular students to

Mr. Thom when they quickly check in with each other midway and at the end of the math period. Even though these station activities are examples of *parallel* co-teaching, Ms. Hernandez believes she also is practicing the *supportive* co-teaching role, because she is supporting Mr. Thom to diagnose and problem solve for particular students.

MS. BARTOLO: MIDDLE SCHOOL ■ CO-TEACHING AND COLLABORATIVEPLANNING

Supportive, Parallel, and Complementary Co-Teaching in English Classes

Ms. Bartolo, the middle level paraeducator that we have been following, continues to comfortably co-teach with both middle level English teachers. In their regularly scheduled planning time, Ms. Cole, Ms. Hendrickson, and Ms. Bartolo decide which co-teaching approaches will be employed in upcoming lessons. Frequently, during the course of a single lesson, Ms. Bartolo will move in and out of the supportive, parallel, and complementary roles. Ms. Bartolo is excited about an upcoming lesson in Ms. Cole's English class: The students will begin reading *Siddhartha* by Hermann Hesse. Ms. Cole explains that she wants her students to acquire or expand their background knowledge about related topics prior to reading the novel. She plans to have students working in teams select from among eight related topics. They are to study their topic, become experts on the topic, and then teach their expert content to the rest of the class. The eight topics from which they will choose to study are (a) Hermann Hesse, (b) origins of the Buddhist religion, (c) practices and beliefs of Buddhism (i.e., Four Noble Truths and Eightfold Path), (d) origins of the Hindu religion, (e) practices and beliefs of Hinduism (Search/Quest for Truth), (f) caste systems (Brahman and others), (g) enlightenment and nirvana, and (h) asceticism (in spirituality).

Ms. Bartolo shares with Ms. Cole the reasons for her excitement. Specifically, Hermann Hesse was one of her favorite authors when she was in school, and her fiancé is a practicing Buddhist from Cambodia. Ms. Bartolo has studied the Buddhist religion and attended numerous temple functions and ceremonies with her fiancé. Ms. Cole is pleased to learn of Ms. Bartolo's interest in the author and experience with Buddhism. They decide to create two groups of the students and parallel co-teach as the students learn and then prepare to share their knowledge in 10- to-15-minute presentations. Ms. Bartolo is assigned to primarily work with the three groups that are studying the biography of Hermann Hesse, the origins of the Buddhist religion, and practices and beliefs of Buddhism. Ms. Cole assumes primary responsibility for working with the other five expert groups.

Ms. Cole begins the class by introducing the topic and the expert group activity. Ms. Bartolo co-teaches in the supportive role as she moves among the students, monitoring their recording of the pertinent information in their language arts journals. Ms. Bartolo co-teaches in the complementary role when she records some of the key points Ms, Cole is explaining on the interactive white board. She paraphrases some of Ms. Cole's statements, and records notes on a transparency of the grading rubric to be used to evaluate the expert group presentations to the class.

Following the introduction and a question-and-answer time, the students self-select their topics and arrange themselves into the expert groups. After 10 minutes, Ms. Bartolo and Ms. Cole move among the groups, reviewing the draft work plans that the student groups have developed. The work plan must identify all members of the group, their role in gathering and presenting information, the use of visual aids, and how they plan to engage the class in activities during their presentation.

The students learn which member of the co-teaching team will primarily monitor their academic and social skill performance as they learn and study their chosen topic. Even though the class has been divided into groups that will work primarily with Ms. Cole or Ms. Bartolo, all groups must share their draft work plan with and receive approval by Ms. Cole before they begin to study and develop their presentation. Any subsequent major revisions to their plan must also be shared with Ms. Cole.

Supportive and Complementary Co-Teaching in Science Class

After the team discussion of each person's strengths and dislikes when working with others and the information about how Ms. Bartolo is co-teaching in the English classes, Ms. Bartolo's role begins to slowly change in the science class. Mr. Ruhan still wants Ms. Bartolo to move among the students in a supportive role, as he feels that her presence assists in keeping them on task academically and behaviorally. In addition, he begins to feel comfortable with Ms. Bartolo functioning in a complementary role as she records major points on the board or a transparency and develops and adds words to the Word Wall in the classroom. When Ms. Bartolo functions in the complementary role, Mr. Ruhan moves from the front of the room and lectures and guides activities from the middle and back of the room. He soon discovers that his presence closer to the students in all parts of the room has a powerful positive effect on their behavior, and he commits to having Ms. Bartolo expand the amount of time she co-teaches in a complementary role. He is beginning to feel that Ms. Bartolo's presence is an asset and not a burden.

Parallel Co-Teaching in the Learning Center

After Ms. Bartolo shares her concern about Bradley (the boy with autism) being isolated from the other students in the learning center, she and Ms. Brinkley jointly decide to switch his location from the back of the learning center to a place closer to where other students are working. Ms. Brinkley tells Ms. Bartolo that she wants her to facilitate peer interactions for Bradley and avoid being "Velcroed" to him. Ms. Brinkley models for Ms. Bartolo how to work with and support Bradley and how to facilitate peer interactions. She commits to continue to do so, as well as observe Ms. Bartolo work with Bradley and provide feedback to her at least once a week for the next two months.

Ms. Bartolo and Ms. Brinkley discuss how Ms. Bartolo's role will expand in the learning center as Bradley gains more independence and also increases his peer interdependence. Ms. Bartolo is intrigued with the peer tutors who are supporting learners who came to the learning center. She laughingly comments that it is clear to her that the students prefer to work with peers rather than adults and that maybe she will lose her job. Ms. Brinkley explains that there is little chance of that because the student interactions need to be monitored and data need to be collected on academic, behavioral, and communication goals for many of the students who attend the learning center. Ms. Bartolo comments that her job continues to evolve and that she enjoys this feature of the job because the changes are all positive and there is no time to get bored as she is always learning and doing new things. Ms. Brinkley quietly celebrates the growth in Ms. Bartolo's confidence, competence, and advocacy for herself and the students with whom she works.

MR. ANDERSON: SECONDARY SCHOOL TEAM CO-TEACHING AND COLLABORATIVE PLANNING

Mr. Anderson, the secondary paraeducator, works with two co-teachers: Mr. Schwab, a science teacher, and Ms. Bennevento, a social studies teacher. Typically, he co-plans twice weekly with the two teachers and his supervisor and a special education teacher, Ms. Clooney. Most weeks, Mr. Anderson works with the science co-teacher in science class on Monday and Wednesday while Ms. Clooney co-teaches in social studies. On the alternate days, Mr. Anderson and Ms. Clooney switch classrooms, with Mr. Anderson working with Ms. Bennevento in social studies class and Ms. Clooney working in the science class.

Adjusting Co-Teaching to Support Student Needs

At this week's planning meeting, the team decides to alter the usual co-teaching routine. Ms. Clooney will be in Mr. Schwab's science class all five days. Mr. Anderson will be in Ms. Bennevento's social studies class Monday through Thursday and then join the science classroom on Friday to become familiar with changes that have been made. The reason for this change is that there are two new students with Individual Education Programs (IEPs) who have just joined Mr. Schwab's science class. Ms. Clooney will observe Garrick, one of the new students whose behaviors trouble Mr. Schwab and other teachers in the school. She then will use the data collected from these observations to assist Garrick's IEP team to develop a behavior support plan to address the behaviors of concern. Ms. Clooney also will help diagnose, develop, and model, through their co-teaching modifications for Shonique, another new student who has moderate disabilities. Mr. Schwab welcomes the idea of Ms. Clooney's support for the entire week. On Friday, Mr. Anderson will join them to become familiar with the behavioral and academic modifications developed by Ms. Clooney and Mr. Schwab that he will be carrying when he returns the following week.

Recently, all four members of the team participated in a school-sponsored inservice training session on two frameworks for thinking about what and how to teach Multiple Intelligences (MI) theory (Armstrong, 2000; Gardner, 1999) and Bloom's taxonomy (Anderson & Krathwohl, 2001; Bloom, Englehart, Furst, Hill, & Krathwohl, 1956). Ms. Bennevento has already learned how to incorporate the various levels of Bloom's revised taxonomy, especially using action words when explaining to children what she expects for learning objectives. Now she is eager to use the MI framework to design how students will engage in learning and show what they know about the U.S. Constitution in the upcoming unit.

She has learned that MI theory assumes that all students possess in different proportions many different intelligences, described in Table 5.4. As part of her discovery process about the value of MI theory, Ms. Bennevento delved into sources that critiqued the theory. For example, she found a book review published in 1999 by Reed Business Information, Inc. (*Publisher's Weekly*) which stated, "Harvard education professor Gardner adds to the list a new naturalist intelligence, which involves attunement to the environment, its flora and fauna. He further proposes that there may be a spiritual or existential intelligence (knowledge of transcendental and cosmic matters), but adds that this awaits scientific verification" (retrieved April 27, 2008, from http://www.amazon.com/Intelligence-Reframed-Multiple-Intelligences-Century/dp/0465026117). And during a Web-assisted seminar with teachers in 1999 in which he was asked about existentialist intelligence, Howard Gardner noted, "We are trying to find good biological evidence for it. I have a chapter on this question in *Intelligence Reframed* (1999) which should be in your book store any day now-Briefly, existential intelligence draws on the human capacity to ask and try

Table 5.4
Definitions of the Multiple Intelligences

1. Verbal/Linguistic	is word oriented; is sensitive to sounds, structures, meanings, and functions of words; may show an affinity to storytelling, writing, reading, and verbal play (e.g., jokes, puns, riddles).
2. Logical/ Mathematical	is concept oriented; has capacity to perceive logical or numerical patterns; has a scientific or numerical nature to discover or test hypotheses.
3. Visual/Spatial	is image and picture oriented; is able to perceive the world visually and to perform transformations on those perceptions; may daydream and demonstrate artistic, designer, or inventive qualities.
4. Musical/Rhythmic	is rhythm and melody oriented; can produce and appreciate rhythm, pitch, timbre, and multiple forms of musical expression; may be animated or calmed by music.
5. Bodily/Kinesthetic	is physically oriented; uses body movements for self-expression (e.g., acting, dancing, mime); excels in athletics, uses touch to interpret the environment, can skillfully handle or produce objects requiring fine-motor abilities.
6. Interpersonal	is socially oriented, has strong mediation and leadership skills, can teach others and discern moods, temperaments, and motivations of people.
7. Intrapersonal	is intuitively oriented, can access and interpret one's own feelings, may be strong-willed or self-motivated, may prefer solitary activities.
8. Naturalist	has capacity to classify nature; has outstanding knowledge of or sensitivity to things that exist in the natural world; has ability to discern patterns in nature.
9. Existentialist	is curious about the "Very Big Questions" such as: Who are we? Where do we come from? Why are we here? What is going to happen to us?

Level of Bloom's Taxonomy (Revised)	Action Verbs
Remembering	Recalling, restating, memorizing, retelling, naming
Understanding	Demonstrating, understanding, summarizing in your own words, giving an example of the concept being learned
Applying	Predicting outcomes, estimating answers, using a formula
Analyzing	Classifying, comparing and contrasting, reorganizing information into categories
Evaluating	Judging, rating, arguing, defending
Synthesizing	Creating, imagining, hypothesizing, inventing, prescribing

Table 5.5
The Levels of Bloom's Taxonomy and Action Verbs Associated With Each Level

to answer Very Big Questions" (Retrieved April 27, 2008, from http://teachers.net/archive/gardner092899.html).

Even with the cautions that Howard Gardner himself has offered to educators, Ms. Bennevento appreciates that MI theory promotes the idea that intelligence is neither one-dimensional nor fixed. She wants to find out for herself to what extent her students might improve in their achievement if she structures her lessons around the concepts. She realizes that identifying and using a person's strength intelligences can motivate and assist that person to learn new or difficult information. In addition, areas can be strengthened when exercised and given an opportunity to develop. Giving students choices to learn and show what they know through their preferred intelligences can motivate and allow students to show their best work.

At the same inservice session, the teachers and paraeducator learned about Bloom's taxonomy of educational objectives or thinking complexity, which ranks thinking into six levels. Table 5.5 shows these six levels along with sample verbs or actions associated with each level of thinking. Remembering and understanding levels of the taxonomy are the launching pads for higher levels of thinking. Historically, teachers often have provided activities or had performance expectations at primarily the remembering and understanding levels, particularly for students eligible for special education or who are learning English. This team has taken to heart the importance of teachers holding high expectations and offering all students the entire range—all six levels—of thinking opportunities.

Supportive and Parallel Co-Teaching in Social Studies

Ms. Bennevento and Mr. Anderson are excited that they will co-teach social studies for four consecutive days. They start a new unit on the U.S. Constitution on Monday, and having the same instructors for the first four days of the unit should provide continuity as students make choices as to how they want to achieve social studies standards in the unit. During their planning meeting, Ms. Bennevento, Ms. Clooney, and Mr. Anderson use what they know about MI theory and Bloom's taxonomy to brainstorm differentiated product options from which the students can select to sho what they learned about the U.S. Constitution. The completed differentiated matrix developed by Ms. Bennevento, Ms. Clooney, and Mr. Anderson appears in Table 5.6.

Table 5.6

Integration of Bloom's Taxonomy and Multiple Intelligences Theory for Lesson Activities

Remembering	Understanding	Applying	Analyzing	Evaluating	Synthesizing
Dimensions—Verbal/Linguistic					
Following pre-assessment of knowledge of related vocabulary terms, develop a dictionary of key terms not previously understood. Include at least 20 items and their definitions.	Describe, in your own words, how a bill becomes a law.		Compare and contrast in writing the U.S. Constitution with one from another country (e.g., South Africa, France, Russia, Chile, the People's Republic of China).	Write an essay of at least 1,000 words explaining which of the first 10 amendments to the Constitution is most important to you and why.	
Dimensions—Visual/Spatial					
	Create a Constitution Handbook of important information from each article. Use your own words. Illustrate each of your key points with a graphic representation (drawn or selected from the Internet).	Draw a political cartoon depicting what a European monarch would have thought about the newly formed democratic constitutional government of the United States.	Compare and contrast, in a PowerPoint® presentation, the U.S. Constitution with a constitution from another country.	Design a visual display to represent the qualities that your ideal Supreme Court justice would possess.	
Dimensions—Logical/Mathematical					
	Develop a timeline of significant events starting with the Declaration of Independence and ending with the adoption of the Constitution by the states.		Compare and contrast in tables or charts two documents: the U.S. Constitution and a constitution from another country.		
Dimensions—Naturalist					
		Write a letter to one of your state representatives sharing an idea on conserving the environment you would like to see become a law.			Develop an environmental conservation proposal you would like to see enacted in our school. Take your proposal to a student council meeting and advocate for its passage.
Dimensions—Musical					
					Develop a rap, poem, or song about the U.S. Constitution. Be prepared to perform your rap, poem, or song in front of the class.

Remembering	Understanding	Applying	Analyzing	Evaluating	Synthesizing
Dimensions—Bodily/Kinesthetic					
	Create and perform a commercial designed to recruit representatives to Congress. Be sure that you include job description, job requirements, and responsibilities for both senators and representatives.		Choreograph and perform an interpretive dance about the Bill of Rights.		Create a board game to assess knowledge and comprehension of the U.S. Constitution. Be sure to include the rules for playing the game.
Dimensions—Intrapersonal					
		Identify 10 ways the Constitution affects your life. Provide an example for each. Be imaginative in how you present the information: poster, PowerPoint®, diary or journal entry, letter to a friend living in another country, essay.		Read the amendments to the Constitution (excluding the Bill of Rights) and select three that are most important to your life. Explain why.	
Dimensions—Interpersonal					
		In a cooperative group of 2 or 3, write and perform a script for a TV police show that illustrates how the fourth amendment is used in real-life situations.	Pretend you are a journalist assigned to interview a real candidate in an upcoming election. Develop your interview questions, research the candidate and his/her positions, and predict how s/he would answer your questions.		
Dimensions—Existentialist					
	In your own words, how might the Constitution define who you are—the kind of person you are?				If all nations used the Constitution, what do you think would happen to humans on the planet Earth?

They agree that students will be required to select three items from the matrix menu to demonstrate their learnings regarding the U.S. Constitution. Of these three choices, only one can be at the knowledge and comprehension levels of Bloom's taxonomy. Students must perform at least one activity alone and at least one with a partner or a group. The decisions that

Ms. Bennevento, Ms. Clooney, and Mr. Anderson made about the first four days of the unit are memorialized in the co-teaching lesson plan shown in Table 5.7. (See Resource H for a blank template.)

Table 5.7
A Four-Day Co-Teaching Lesson Plan for Mr. Anderson's Team

Date: December 13 through December 16   **Co-Teachers:** Ms. Bennevento, Mr. Anderson

Content Area(s): Social Studies   **(Names)** Ms. Clooney (planning and debriefing only)

Lesson Objectives: Analyze the principles, ideals, and rights within the U.S. Constitution.

Content Standards Addressed: Civics and Government 5.1.9 E.[3]

Underline the Co-Teaching Approach(es) Used:

Supportive   Parallel   Complementary   Team Teaching

What is the room arrangement? Will other spaces outside of the classroom be used?

Centers and stations arranged within the room.

If necessary, students can access additional computers in the library/media center.

What materials do the co-teachers need?

Task directions	Grading rubrics	LCD projector
Three-choice work plan worksheets	Chart paper	List of Web sites
Colored markers	Text-to-speech software	Musical instruments
iPod with speakers	Texts with various reading levels	

How do co-teachers assess student learning?

Review and approve each student's three-choice work plan.

Review each student's individual assessment of group behavior.

Review cooperative group team assessments.

Apply grading and presentation rubrics.

Review co-teacher observations.

What specific supports, aids, or services do select students need?

We do not believe that additional supports and services are needed because of the range of reading materials, use of technology, use of MI theory, and the availability of peer and adult support. We will monitor student progress and provide additional supports if and when necessary.

---

3. PA. Civics and Government Standards. Download available http://www.pde.state.pa.us/stateboard_ed/cwp/view.asp?Q=76716

What does each co-teacher do before, during, and after the lesson?

Co-Teacher Name:	Bennevento	Anderson	Clooney
What are the specific tasks that I do BEFORE the lesson?	Brainstorm integrated MI theory and Bloom's taxonomy matrix. Brainstorm list of varied product options. (See Table 5.6.) Identify and gather varied materials. Set up stations. Prepare task direction sheet, grading rubric, and three-choice student worksheet.	Brainstorm integrated MI theory and Bloom's taxonomy matrix. Brainstorm varied product options. Set up stations.	Brainstorm integrated MI theory and Bloom's taxonomy matrix. Brainstorm list of Web resources and varied product options. Identify and gather varied materials.
What are the specific tasks that I do DURING the lesson?	Explain academic and social task and criteria for success. Approve individual student plans that identify their three product options. Primarily work at stations with students who have selected verbal/linguistic, mathematical/logical, naturalist, interpersonal, and intrapersonal options. (Parallel co-teaching)	Monitor students as they record pertinent information in their journals. (Supportive) Work with students at stations who have selected visual/spatial, kinesthetic, and musical options. (Parallel)	
What are the specific tasks that I do AFTER the lesson?	Review and grade student products. Meet with Ms. Clooney to review student products and suggest additional modifications.		Meet with Ms. Bennevento to review student products and suggest additional modifications.

Where, when, and how do co-teachers debrief and evaluate the outcomes of the lesson?

Ms. Bennevento and Mr. Anderson will meet informally before and after class on Monday, Tuesday, Wednesday, and Thursday to discuss what went well and what can be done to improve the lesson. At the formal regularly scheduled meeting, all three will discuss student progress, review products, assign future groups, and discuss whether or not additional supports are needed for any student.

The lesson plan identifies which co-teaching approaches the co-teachers plan to use, what each person does before, during, and after the lesson, and when and where they will reflect and debrief. Before the lesson, Ms. Bennevento and Ms. Clooney gather various materials and items that the students can use to access information and demonstrate their learning. During the lesson, Ms. Bennevento approves each student's three product selections. After selections are approved, Mr. Anderson works primarily with students who have selected visual/spatial, musical, and bodily-kinesthetic product options, because these MI areas are his relative strength areas. Ms. Bennevento assumes primary responsibility for the other MI product areas, because they more closely match her strength intelligence areas. After the lesson each day, Ms. Bennevento and Mr. Anderson meet briefly to examine student work and agree on adjustments for the next day. They also meet with Ms. Clooney at their regular team meeting times.

■ SUMMARY

Take a moment to reflect on what you have read and learned in this chapter. Did you discover ways that a paraeducator can work as a co-teacher in today's classrooms? Have you found yourself using any of the co-teaching approaches that paraeducators are most likely to experience as they help students in the classroom? In what ways have you guided instruction by using a co-teaching lesson plan format? Can you imagine how you might use the format in future lessons? Do you hear yourself using the terminology of action words to describe the various levels of comprehension your students show you? In what ways do you notice that you already use the variety of multiple intelligences in your work with children and youths?

Were you able to see yourself in the elementary, middle, and/or secondary school scenarios? Can you imagine yourself using strategies similar to those used by the paraeducators in the scenarios? In what ways might you share what you now know about co-teaching and its variations with your supervising teachers or with fellow teachers and paraeducators? In what ways might this help increase the effectiveness of how educators, yourself included, work together in the same classroom to support students? Our hope is that you now have a number of ideas about how you might stretch your own opportunities to plan for and engage in co-teaching with a variety of people to benefit the students of your school. The bottom line is that you should be feeling empowered to take meaningful action in your role!

Support Systems for Paraeducators' Success

Professional Development, Supervision, and Logistical Support

Figure 6.1
Paraeducators'
Questions About
Professional
Development

Image created by Jodie Beecher.

We realize that paraeducators have many concerns about support systems. In this chapter we examine the research and best practices on professional development, supervision, and logistical support that promote paraeducators' success on the job. We propose a cycle for melding professional development and supervision for paraeducators' continuous self-improvement. As in previous chapters, you will revisit the paraeducators introduced in Chapter 2, this time to judge how successful their teams have been at providing professional development, supervision, and logistical support. Guiding questions for this chapter are:

- What professional development do paraeducators need, and what are the skills required for paraeducators?
- What are the approaches to professional development for paraeducators?
- What should paraeducators expect from teachers in terms of supervision and coaching?
- What are dimensions of effective supervision for paraeducators?
- What is logistical support? What logistical supports help paraeducators to be welcomed and supported in their jobs?

■ PROFESSIONAL DEVELOPMENT AND THE SKILLS REQUIRED FOR PARAEDUCATORS

Reflecting upon a predominant way in which schools provide special education support to students with identified disabilities, Mueller (2002) laments, "We have developed a service delivery system that depends heavily on relatively untrained . . . staff members to provide complex instructional and behavioral programs to our most challenging students" (p. 64). Mueller refers to this phenomenon as the *paraprofessional paradox.* Clearly, no one in education wants our valuable paraeducators to be left untrained or undertrained to do the complex jobs they are asked to perform daily. Administrators, teachers, and paraeducators can avoid this paradox by providing adequate preparation and supervision of paraeducators. The literature is rich in comprehensive paraeducator development options and the impact on paraeducators' work with K–12 learners (see Resource I for a list of professional development opportunities, materials, and Web sites). What follows is a summary of some of the key areas in which paraeducators should expect professional development as well as descriptions of various ways in which paraeducators can receive training.

■ THE APPROACHES TO PROFESSIONAL DEVELOPMENT FOR PARAEDUCATORS

More now than ever, paraeducators are being held to high standards with regard to knowledge of academic content and the dispositions and skills they are expected to exhibit in their daily work. Sources of knowledge and skill requirements come from at least three sources: federal legislation, analyses of paraeducator job descriptions or duties, and standards of professional organizations.

What the Law Requires

Both the Individuals with Disabilities Education Improvement Act (IDEIA) and the No Child Left Behind Act (NCLB) set legal requirements for what paraeducators must know as well as define some restriction on their role in the classroom. IDEIA, for example, requires each state to establish standards to ensure all paraeducators are adequately trained to do the job for which they are hired. If adequately trained and supervised, a paraeducator may *assist* in serving students eligible for special education.

> You can easily access paraeducator standards, state-by-state, from the PAR^{2}A Center (Paraprofessional Resource and Research Center) Web site at www.paracenter.org.

NCLB contains educational requirements that can be satisfied by schooling (i.e., two years or 48 semester units of college—an associate's degree) or a passing score on a state-approved exam. NCLB also requires paraeducators to demonstrate skill in the following areas: the use of general instructional techniques and methods, the use of instructional techniques and methods for assisting in literacy and math, behavior management and behavior support skills, legal and ethical practices, and adult interpersonal communication and teamwork skills.

NCLB further specifies that paraeducator support is to *supplement* instruction provided by a fully qualified teacher. While professional educators are responsible for developing lesson plans and adaptations, paraeducators are responsible for being able to *carry out* instruction according to the lesson plans.

What a Job Analysis Suggests

To help form a process to assess paraeducator competence, Nancy French (2003), the founder and former executive director of the PAR^{2}A Center, offers two self-assessment inventories for paraeducators to use. One inventory assesses potential paraeducator responsibilities in a classroom or school (i.e., delivery of instruction, activity preparation, supervision of groups of students, behavior management, ethics, team participation and membership, clerical work, home school communication, and other special education duties). The other inventory examines the paraeducator's confidence on the same items. Results of the two inventories can inform paraeducators as to both what their immediate job responsibilities are and for which responsibilities they need further instruction (i.e., those for which they are not confident).

Table 6.1 shows "An Inventory of Paraeducator Preparedness" based upon job elements identified by and included in both of the French (2003) inventories. This inventory is offered as a starting point for paraeducators to assess their own level of perceived preparedness and skills on basic classroom and school duties. This inventory can be used in various ways. The self-rating results can guide paraeducators' supervisors to determine

Table 6.1

An Inventory of Paraeducator Preparedness

Job Responsibility	Rating Unprepared → Highly Skilled			
	1	**2**	**3**	**4**
Delivery of Instruction				
1. Observe and record student progress in academic areas.				
2. Assist to differentiate instruction.				
3. Help students in drill and practice (e.g., vocabulary, math facts).				
4. Help students use computers and software.				
5. Engage in supportive, parallel, complementary, and team teaching co-teaching as requested by supervising teachers.				
Activity Preparation and Follow-Up				
6. Distribute supplies, materials, and books to students.				
7. Collect completed work from students.				
8. Operate equipment (e.g., tape recorders, DVD, LCD and document projectors).				
Supervising Groups				
9. Supervise students during lunch or recess.				
10. Escort groups to library, gym, or bathroom.				
Behavior Management				
11. Implement classroom discipline system.				
12. Observe and chart individual student behavior.				
Ethics				
13. Maintain confidentiality of information.				
14. Respect privacy of students and their families.				
15. Respect dignity and rights of every child (e.g., use person-first, disability-second language).				
16. Maintain composure and emotional control when working with students.				
Team Participation				
17. Contribute ideas in team meetings.				
18. Engage in roles (e.g., timekeeper, encourager) as needed or requested during a meeting.				
Clerical				
19. Score objective tests and enter data in grade book.				
20. Organize, file, and copy teaching or assessment materials.				

Adapted from French, N. (2003). Management of paraeducators. In A. L. Pickett & K. Gerlach (Eds.). *Supervising paraeducators in school settings: A team approach* (2nd ed.). Austin, TX: PRO-ED. Reprinted with permission.

professional development activities for individuals or groups of para-educators. Results also can be used to guide individual paraeducators toward self-selected professional development activities. The main skill areas shown in the table are self-evident.

Note that it is not necessary to use the exact items listed in Table 6.1 or other inventories in this book, such as the collaborative teaming checklists offered in Chapter 4. The idea is to conduct an analysis of the day-to-day required duties and actions of a paraeducator as well as the stated requirements in the paraeducator's job description in order to determine what the paraeducator needs to know and learn to do. A clear description and analysis of the functions a paraeducator's job entails and those it does not are especially important for paraeducators who co-teach, because co-teaching can require quite complex instructional, behavior management, assessment, ethical, and interpersonal behaviors and responsibilities.

What Standards of Professional Organizations Suggest

Paraeducator skills standards also can help supervisors and para-educators in selecting professional development activities.

One advantage of starting to build professional development for paraeducators around skills standards is that standards tend to focus training on content that should positively affect students. For example, one skill area concerns general education instructional techniques and methods and includes such skills as carrying out individual adaptation plans and changing and managing materials according to a plan. Another skill group concerns management and support skills, focusing on skills such as demonstrating how to observe and record behaviors for use in functional assessments. Paraeducators whose professional development activities help them work with children are more likely to be satisfied on the job.

> One recently formulated set of skill standards that incorporates the subject matter and instructional requirements for paraeducators set out in the No Child Left Behind Act can be found in the electronic library of the PAR²A Center (www.paracenter.org/PARACenter/library).

The Council for Exceptional Children (CEC) publication, *What Every Special Educator Must Know: Ethics, Standards, and Guidelines for Special Educators (2003)*, identifies standards of conduct for special educators and paraeducators. Emphasized in this document are ethical standards, explicitly stated in Standard 9 for paraeducators. Table 6.2 summarizes the CEC ethical standards in a format similar to Table 6.1 so that it too can be used as a self-assessment inventory.

No matter what the source of ethical standards, at a minimum they usually address at least three topics: confidentiality, reporting suspicions of abuse, and responsible treatment of children. Let's take a moment to examine each one of these topics, starting with confidentiality. Paraeducators are expected at all times to protect the anonymity of students; that is, to keep student information private. For instance, paraeducators are to share the data they collect or the observations they have about students with others only on a "need to know basis." This means that only the

Table 6.2
A Paraeducator
Self-Assessment
Checklist for
Professional Ethical
Practices

Note: Place a check under the Yes I can! column for each statement that is true at this point.	Yes I Can!
Knowledge: "I know about…"	
ethical practices for confidential communication about individuals with exceptional learning needs.	_____
personal cultural biases and differences that affect my ability to work with others.	_____
Skills: "I can/will…"	
perform responsibilities as directed in a manner consistent with laws and policies.	_____
follow instructions of the professional.	_____
engage in problem solving, flexible thinking, conflict management techniques, and analysis of personal strengths and preference.	_____
act as a role model for individuals with exceptional learning needs.	_____
assist learners in achieving their highest potential.	_____
separate personal issues from my responsibilities as a paraeducator.	_____
exercise objective and prudent judgment.	_____
maintain a high level of competence and integrity.	_____
demonstrate proficiency in academic skills, including oral and written communication, and engage in activities to increase my own knowledge and skills.	_____
engage in self-assessment and accept and use constructive feedback.	_____
demonstrate ethical practices as guided by the CEC Code of Ethics and other standards and policies.	_____

Adapted from Standard 9 of the Standards for Professionals Serving Individuals with Exceptional Learning Needs published in Council for Exceptional Children (2003). *What Every Special Educator Must Know: Ethics, Standards, and Guidelines for Special Educators* (5th ed.) ©The Council for Exceptional Children. Reprinted with permission.

teachers, specialists, and administrators who need to know the information are provided with the data collected by paraeducators. This confidentiality agreement extends to all educational and medical records about the child or the family that the paraeducator might read.

Second, paraeducators are required to conduct themselves within the guidelines of responsible adults in the lives of children. This means they must report suspected incidents of child abuse or inappropriate actions toward children, wherever such incidents are observed. Third, paraeducators are expected to live by the same rule that guides medical professionals, *primum non nocere*—first, do no harm. It is a good practice to always ask if the action you intend to take might in any way possibly result in emotional or physical distress or harm to the child. If you think it might, then don't do it! Ask for an alternative!

WHAT PARAEDUCATORS ■
SHOULD EXPECT FROM TEACHERS
IN TERMS OF SUPERVISION AND COACHING

Paraeducators can expect to receive professional development in a variety of ways, probably the most common being on-the-job training. More formal training programs also have been developed by state departments of education, school districts, and universities. What follows are descriptions and examples of both on-the-job and more formal professional development.

On-the-Job Training

On-the-job training often is student-specific or job-specific. For example, if a paraeducator is hired to provide behavior support for students, the focus of training likely will be, at least initially, on behavior management and positive behavior support techniques. If a paraeducator is hired to provide general support as a co-teacher in content area classes, general instructional methods and methods specific to the content area (e.g., math instruction, reading instruction) will be priority areas for professional development. On-the-job training takes many forms. It can involve modeling on the part of teachers of what to do with students, detailed explanation of a task and demonstrations on video or DVD, or constructive feedback on observed delivery of instruction or interventions. It can take the form of reading materials or Web sites to which the paraeducator is directed for information and procedures. On-the-job training can be more structured and formal in nature, as described in the next section.

Formal Professional Development Programs

With the increased number of paraeducators being hired over the past couple of decades to support students in general education, some school districts have been proactive and established well-developed paraeducator professional training programs as part of their district's comprehensive professional development plan. Other districts, compelled by the recent NCLB and IDEIA mandates that articulate educational requirements for paraeducators, have responded by organizing within-district professional development programs to assure their state departments of education that their paraeducators are adequately trained and supervised to qualify to deliver the special education and related services for which they were hired.

More formal professional development for paraeducators may take the form of a job-embedded inservice training series or an ongoing regular study group. An example of a state-supported job-embedded study group is the Paraprofessionals as Partners Study Group, a collaborative effort between the Connecticut State Education Resource Center (SERC) and the Connecticut chapter of the America Federation of Teachers (AFT). The curriculum for the study group includes core skills required by NCLB and many of the skills identified in Table 6.1 (Fenn, 2005; Fenn & White, 2007.

The SERC materials spell out procedures for establishing a study group, choosing a facilitator, and conducting the study activities. They also identify needed administrative support such as arranging for the appropriate space and times for paraeducators to meet during their school day, allowing for released time for a facilitator to prepare for the group meetings, and providing training materials for the meetings. SERC support consists of annual statewide conference time for paraeducators to be trained as study group facilitators, on-site SERC consultation support, access to the SERC library, and specific training for various aspects of study group facilitation.

In most states, there are additional professional development opportunities such as local or regional conferences. The topics of the conference typically are designed for paraeducators to acquire a wide variety of knowledge, skills, and strategies. Topics can focus on inclusive education, collaboration and co-teaching, behavior management and positive behavior supports, literacy strategies, innovations in math instructions, and Response to Intervention (RtI) models that paraeducators can attend, preferably with their supervising teacher or team. We are strong advocates of teams attending professional development opportunities, so that they share the conceptual frameworks and techniques they learn together. This allows for a shared vocabulary for discussing students and interventions and for brainstorming ways in which to apply what was learned when back on the school site.

■ DIMENSIONS OF EFFECTIVE SUPERVISION FOR PARAEDUCATORS

As already mentioned, NCLB and IDEIA require that personnel hired as paraeducators work under the supervision of at least one licensed or certificated professional such as a special educator, classroom teacher, certified reading specialist, speech and language pathologist, or other related services personnel such as an occupational or physical therapist. With that said, what should a paraeducator expect for supervision?

What Supervision Is and Is Not

It has been said that half of knowing what something *is* consists of knowing what it is *not*. What, then, does *not* represent quality supervision of a paraeducator? Supervision is *not* expecting a paraeducator to learn how to perform the job on his or her own, focusing only on a paraeducator's errors, or leaving a paraeducator alone to design and deliver instruction. In fact, NCLB specifies that all paraeducators who provide instruction must work under direct supervision of a fully qualified teacher. It is actually illegal for a paraeducator to be the sole or primary service provider for a student, because this violates the student's right to a free and appropriate public education from a highly qualified professional educator.

What, then, *is* quality supervision? At the very least, it is ensuring that paraeducators have the knowledge and skills to do the job based upon periodic observations of their performance on the job. Quality supervision is having clear communication systems and face-to-face time to transmit information and provide modeling, coaching, and constructive feedback to improve instruction and student learning.

In the United States, how well are we providing quality supervision of paraeducators? Research indicates that the majority of beginning teachers are responsible for scheduling and supervising at least one paraeducator. Yet, most report being "unsure of themselves as they discovered this additional, unexpected aspect of their jobs" (Gehrke & Murri, 2006, p. 186), and they often do not plan with their paraeducators. For example, French (2001) found that of the 321 teachers she studied, fewer than 30% systematically planned with their paraeducator.

However, in an earlier (1999) study, French found that teachers who do provide quality supervision of their paraeducators experience high satisfaction with their paraeducators' work. These teachers "regard the work that paraeducators do as necessary to their success and to the success of their students" (p. 71), and they notice that "the presence of paraeducators doubles the amount of instructional time available during school hours" (p. 73). The extra effort of supervision is well worth it!

French (2008b) suggests that teachers who work with paraeducators will be more confident and satisfied with the support paraeducators provide if they engage in at least seven sets of supervisory behaviors:

1. Introduce paraeducators to the school and the expectations of the job.

2. Plan lessons and adaptations for the paraeducators to follow.

3. Schedule paraeducator time.

4. Delegate responsibilities to paraeducators.

5. Provide ongoing on-the-job training.

6. Observe and monitor paraeducators' performance.

7. Communicate and deal with conflict.

Melding Supervision and Professional Development: A Cyclical Growth Model for Paraeducators

We advocate a partnership approach to the supervision and professional development of paraeducators whereby teachers develop their own leadership and mentoring skills while assisting paraeducators to negotiate their job descriptions and gain competence and confidence in discharging their duties. Figure 6.2 offers a cyclical model teachers can use to meld supervision and professional development to support the continuous self-improvement of paraeducators. Notice that this model assumes that the supervising teachers are expected to observe, monitor, and assess the performance of paraeducators. The model also assumes that some standards of professional performance—national, state, or local—are used to guide a collaborative development and implementation of professional development (on-the-job training and/or formal training such as workshops, coursework, and inservice participation). The model also assumes that this is an ongoing recursive process. Thus, the model is conceptualized and

Figure 6.2
A Cyclical Model for Paraeducators' Continuous Self-Improvement

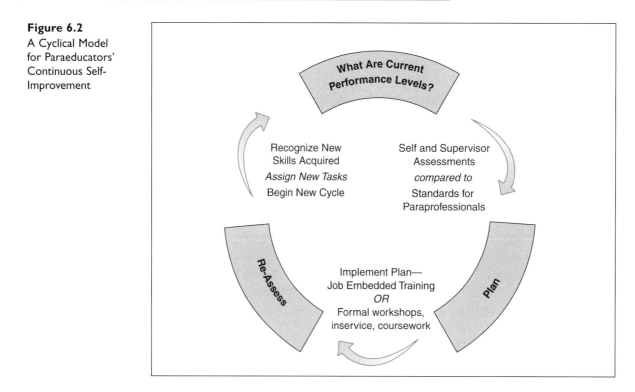

represented in Figure 6.2 as a cycle, indicating that professional development is a life-long learning process.

■ WHAT LOGISTICAL SUPPORT IS, AND WHAT LOGISTICAL SUPPORTS HELP PARAEDUCATORS TO BE WELCOMED AND SUPPORTED IN THEIR JOBS

Paraeducators may not be the best-paid of a school's educational staff. However, they perform, under teacher supervision, essential tasks that support student learning and success. As key contributors to the school community, they are entitled to logistical support that will enable them to be genuine, contributing members of the school community. What does logistical support mean? The *Oxford English Dictionary* traces the meaning of the term "logistics" to a branch of military science having to do with procuring and delivering resources (e.g., material, personnel) in a time-related fashion to keep things operating. In terms of schooling and logistical support for school personnel, logistical support could be considered anything that is provided to make a paraeducator knowledgeable about the school community or better able to function in the job within a school. Logistical support could include provisions or actions that make a paraeducator welcomed within a school and district.

Clearly, professional development and supervision are important logistical supports, ones that already have been discussed in this chapter. Other logistical supports for paraeducators are such things as ensuring that each paraeducator is introduced as a team member to faculty, administrators, custodial and food service staff, parents, and students; assigning each paraeducator a school e-mail address and mailbox; having a place for paraeducators to store their personal items and the instructional materials they use with students; including paraeducators when issuing invitations to professional and personal (e.g., baby showers, luncheons) school functions; and providing them an orientation to school policies and procedures as well as job tasks and responsibilities. What other important logistical supports can you think of?

Sometimes, the elements of a paraeducator's job description or the task demands of a particular paraeducator's assignments reveal the need for other types of logistical support. For example, a paraeducator who is assigned to assist in managing a computer lab will have logistical needs related to computer and software use such as logon security passwords and software specification.

THINKING ABOUT THE EXAMPLES ■

Recall how the paraeducators—Ms. Hernandez, Ms. Bartolo, and Mr. Anderson—and their teams have been working together. You'll remember that each team, in their working relationships, has or has not addressed the dimensions of professional development, supervision, and logistical support discussed in this chapter. As you read through a recap of each scenario below, ask yourself, "What professional development did each paraeducator need? "What type of supervision did each paraeducator receive?" "Can I detect logistical supports that helped each paraeducator feel welcomed and supported on the job?" Then consider whether or not each of the paraeducators is experiencing the kind of professional development, supervision, and logistical support you think would be most helpful given the situations described. What could the team do to improve training, supervision, and support?

MS. HERNANDEZ: ELEMENTARY ■
SCHOOL PARAEDUCATOR EXAMPLE
OF PROFESSIONAL DEVELOPMENT,
SUPERVISION, AND LOGISTICAL SUPPORT

When Ms. Hernandez was hired to be a paraeducator at Chaparral Valley Elementary, she found herself in the enviable position of being invited to and attending, as member of a school team, a formal professional development experience. She and her teammates spent three days learning about inclusive education and the Response to Intervention approach to assisting students early, before they failed.

Professional development also is evidenced by the district's practice of having a reduced teacher schedule on Wednesdays, when students leave at noon rather than 2:30 so staff can meet, plan, and engage in professional development. Once a month, on this student early release Wednesday, the entire Chaparral Valley Elementary staff comes together for a *lunch and learn* professional development and social hour. Paraeducators are invited to attend. Because the principal has arranged for Ms. Hernandez's workday to extend through this lunchtime, she can benefit from attending these school-wide training opportunities while being compensated monetarily. She appreciates this natural and fun way of receiving professional development and the logistical support of being paid to learn and enjoy the sense of community that characterizes these *lunch and learn* events. It was at one of these *lunch and learn* events that she learned about the SODAS problem-solving format (see Resource G) that she and many other teachers have found so valuable.

Ms. Hernandez receives on-the-job training in three ways. First, she receives informal on-the-job training through the weekly scheduled supervision provided by her special educator, Melony Helprin, and the school's reading specialist, Wanda Waldrich. On Wednesday mornings Melony takes Ms. Hernandez's place teaching math for the first half hour in order to monitor student progress on math IEP goals. This gives Ms. Hernandez time to attend, with other literacy tutors, trainings offered by Wanda on new literacy materials and programs. In the second half of this math instruction hour, Melony meets with Ms. Hernandez to examine progress data Ms. Hernandez has collected for students with IEPs and plans, with Ms. Hernandez, next steps for the following week's instructional support.

A second way in which Ms. Hernandez receives on-the-job training is through the structured conversations that occur at the lunchtime collaborative planning meetings among the second and third grades' BRITE *differentiated literacy* teams that occur on all Wednesdays except the *lunch and learn* Wednesdays. For 30 minutes of each grade-level meeting, Ms. Hernandez's team members examine student data from the *differentiated literacy group time* and adjust instructional methods and assign students to new groups, based upon each student's progress. If Ms. Hernandez needs to learn to use a new instructional material or apply a new teaching technique, the team figures out how she will be provided with that information and training.

A third way Ms. Hernandez receives informal on-the-job training is through the ongoing daily modeling and coaching she receives from the second- and third-grade classroom teachers with whom she co-teaches during each grade's *homeroom language arts time*. For example, in Ms. Prada's dual immersion second-grade classroom, Ms. Prada e-mails Ms. Hernandez the instructions for her daily assignments in advance, in time for Ms. Hernandez to review them, ask questions, and come prepared to work with students. Ms. Hernandez considers this embedded form of professional development among the most useful, because she can talk with the classroom teacher to fine-tune and receive immediate feedback on her instruction.

■ MS. BARTOLO: MIDDLE SCHOOL PARAEDUCATOR EXAMPLE OF PROFESSIONAL DEVELOPMENT, SUPERVISION, AND LOGISTICAL SUPPORT

When Ms. Bartolo was hired as a paraeducator, she received a very informal and brief orientation to her job responsibilities but no up-front professional development. From conversations with other paraeducators, she learned that this was not uncommon. She was left to figure out on her own what she was to do in her three co-teaching assignments, how she was to work with Bradley—a young boy with autism with whom she was assigned to work in the learning center—and how she was to execute clerical responsibilities in the office of the Director of Special Education.

You may recall that Ms. Bartolo's hardest and least favorite assignment was co-teaching with a new science teacher, Mr. Ruhan. To Ms. Bartolo, Mr. Ruhan seemed to be unsure of the curriculum and his teaching and not especially welcoming of her presence in the class. Initially she was not allowed to circulate and assist students; instead, she was told to sit at a student's desk and take notes of Mr. Ruhan's lectures, which she then copied and distributed to students whose IEPs stated that they needed this accommodation in order to access the content. After several months and several meetings between Mr. Ruhan, Ms. Bartolo, her supervisor, and the two English teachers with whom Ms. Bartolo co-taught, Mr. Ruhan had a better idea of how to work with Ms. Bartolo. Her role in science classes gradually grew into co-teaching using the supportive and complementary co-teaching approaches.

In terms of supervision and coaching, Ms. Bartolo was assigned a special education supervisor, Ms. Brinkley—who was knowledgeable and experienced but overwhelmed with her own many responsibilities and new major assignments (e.g., the learning center, training peer tutors). Consequently, Ms. Bartolo did not receive the supervision and coaching she would have liked and needed. Nor did she have a written job description. In the absence of her supervisor's leadership, Ms. Bartolo took matters into her own hands. With the help of her co-teachers in English, she drafted a job description, which Ms. Brinkley edited, adopted, and presented to all of Ms. Bartolo's co-teachers. This helped Ms. Bartolo a great deal in clarifying for Mr. Ruhan how a paraeducator could effectively work in a classroom. Ms. Brinkley eventually scheduled weekly planning time with Ms. Bartolo outside of Ms. Bartolo's contracted hours, but for which she was compensated with equivalent release time.

With regard to Bradley, the student with autism, Ms. Bartolo received no explanation of his special needs and no training on how she was to support him. Initially, she and Bradley were assigned to an isolated corner of the learning center. Because of Ms. Bartolo's self-advocacy for training, she eventually was provided with instruction, modeling, and coaching on how to work with this student. The net result was that she felt confident and competent about how best to support Bradley, and she was able to move him out of the corner where he worked alone to learning alongside peers in the learning center.

Ms. Bartolo was fortunate that two of the three teachers with whom she was assigned to co-teach were veteran English teachers. Additionally, both English teachers, Ms. Cole and Ms. Hendrickson, had prior co-teaching experience with paraeducators. To facilitate Ms. Bartolo's co-teaching responsibilities, the three of them used the roles and responsibility matrix (see Table 3.5 or Resource A) to make some initial decisions about how they would work together. In both English classes, Ms. Bartolo was encouraged to circulate among and support all of the students, not just the students with IEPs. In this way, she was engaging in a supportive co-teaching role. Ms. Hendrickson and Ms. Cole assured her that she would expand her role to other forms of co-teaching as she grew into her job. Ms. Hendrickson and Ms. Cole invited Ms. Bartolo to their weekly 30-minute planning meetings and they encouraged her to access Web-based resources for paraeducators (e.g., Fenn, 2005), which she did. These professional development opportunities assisted Ms. Bartolo to expand her co-teaching roles to include the parallel and complementary co-teaching approaches.

■ MR. ANDERSON: SECONDARY SCHOOL PARAEDUCATOR EXAMPLE OF PROFESSIONAL DEVELOPMENT, SUPERVISION, AND LOGISTICAL SUPPORT

Mr. Anderson, a secondary paraeducator who is studying to be a teacher, considers himself fortunate to work in a school where the principal demonstrates visionary leadership through her avid promotion of an inclusive vision, commitment to building capacity among staff, conscious allocation and re-allocation of resources and incentives, and collaboratively engaging faculty and staff in action planning. When we first met Mr. Anderson in Chapter 2, he was entering his fourth year of co-teaching with Mr. Schwab, a science teacher; Ms. Bennevento, a social studies teacher; and Ms. Clooney, a special educator and his primary supervisor. For supervision and professional development, over these four years Mr. Anderson has received ongoing support and coaching from his highly skilled and collaborative co-teachers. He also receives regular direct supervision from Ms. Clooney. He appreciates that, when it comes time for his performance evaluations, she solicits input not only from his co-teachers but from him as well.

Four days a week, at the start of the day, Mr. Schwab and Ms. Bennevento meet briefly (for 20 minutes) with Ms. Clooney, Mr. Anderson's supervising special educator, to plan instruction and talk about students. Mr. Anderson joins them on two of these four days, as this is during his scheduled day. The meetings are always effective and efficient, because they follow closely the collaborative teaming process described in Chapter 4. To improve and celebrate their collaborative behaviors, the team periodically assesses their skills by using the "Are We Really a Collaborative Team?" checklist found as Resource F and shown in Figure 4.4 for Mr. Anderson's team. Mr. Anderson considers these meetings to be the best embedded professional development and supervision that he could receive.

With regard to formal professional development and job clarification, from the beginning of his employment, Mr. Anderson was provided with a detailed job description (see Table 3.6) and well-established professional development experiences. Namely, he takes part in the district's annual two-day summer orientation seminar for paraeducators and the once-a-month formal paraeducator trainings that are designed specifically to address the paraeducators' collective assessed needs. Mr. Anderson and other paraeducators also are invited to attend staff development designed for the certificated teachers, although they are not compensated for training that is outside of their contracted hours. To date, Mr. Anderson has attended training on inclusive education, cooperative group learning, co-teaching, positive behavioral supports, and differentiation of instruction. His co-teaching team also attended a training that they requested and that the district supported them all to attend, in collaborative teaming and the use of Multiple Intelligences theory to differentiate instruction based upon students' preferred intelligences.

SUMMARY AND YOUR NEXT STEPS ■

What did you detect in the three scenarios about the presence or absence of quality professional development, supervision, and logistical support for these elementary, middle, and secondary school paraeducators? Put yourself in the shoes of these three paraeducators. What advice would you give to your team about how to improve the professional development, supervision, and logistical support? What was done well? What compliments might you offer the team members or administrators for providing the professional development, supervision, or logistical support?

In what ways has this chapter helped you to identify the next steps that you, your school, or your district could take to meet the NCLB and IDEIA aims of ensuring your school's paraeducators are highly qualified through quality, ongoing professional development and supervision? In what ways has the information in this chapter led you to think of logistical actions that you, your school, or your district could take to help you or your paraeducators feel highly welcomed and valued?

7

Paraeducators

*Collaborative Members
of Inclusive Teams*

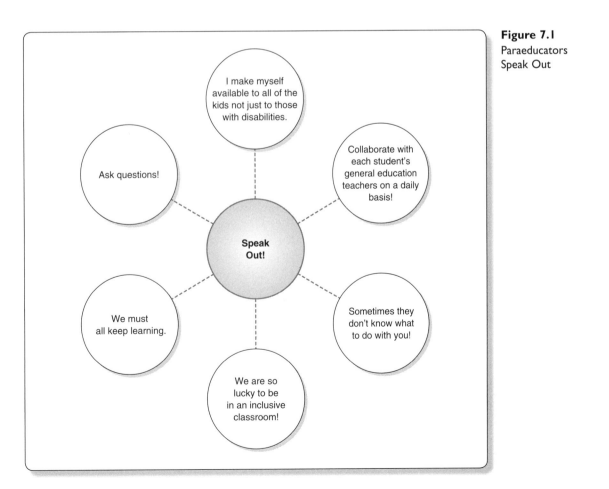

Figure 7.1
Paraeducators
Speak Out

93

We address the following guiding questions in this chapter.

- What do paraeducators say about their work in co-taught classrooms?
- What does a national study of paraeducators in inclusive classrooms say about common issues and emerging roles for paraeducators? What suggestions do the paraeducators in this study offer to other paraeducators?
- Ms. Hernandez, Ms. Bartolo, and Mr. Anderson: What additional advice do they offer?

■ OPINIONS AND ADVICE FROM PARAEDUCATORS IN CO-TAUGHT CLASSROOMS

There are many co-teaching teams where paraeducators are included, valued, and supervised as they work to help differentiate instruction for students with diverse needs. For example, we (the authors) documented experiences of co-teaching teams in California, where we met Ms. Andrea, and in New Mexico, where we met Ms. Sheila.

Ms. Sheila's Experience

Ms. Sheila is a paraeducator in an inclusive middle school in Albuquerque, New Mexico. Ms. Sheila's experience illustrates that paraeducators can and, in schools across the country, do receive adequate preparation as well as the opportunity to collaboratively plan for instruction to meet particular student needs.

> These paraeducators were filmed working in their classrooms and collaboratively planning and/or co-teaching—here we describe part of Ms. Sheila's experience as seen in the Thousand, Villa, Nevin, and Harris (2007) video and DVD and Ms. Andrea's experience as seen in the Villa, Thousand, Nevin, and Harris (2008) video and DVD.

When you meet Ms. Sheila, she has already participated with the entire school staff in a professional development program on how to adapt lesson demands to meet the instructional needs of various learners (Thousand, Villa, & Nevin, 2007). You see her actively contributing in a meeting where the language arts teacher, the inclusion facilitator for the school, and several other members of the support team for a particular student (Debra) are planning for an upcoming lesson. The team solicits Ms. Sheila's opinion, and Ms. Sheila readily shares her perceptions and observations about the Debra's strengths and preferences for working with peers rather than adults.

During the lesson, Debra can be observed as she works alongside a classmate to complete a guided summary of characterizations within a story being read in the language arts class for which we saw Ms. Sheila contribute to the planning. Debra engages in a small group discussion during the lesson. This allows her to rehearse answers which she can then share with the larger class. Ms. Sheila created the visual representation of the daily schedule that sits on Debra's desk as a visual aid for her to keep track of what is next on the agenda. During the lesson, Ms. Sheila is not obviously present. In fact, she and other paraeducators in this school are careful not to hover around students with disabilities or interfere with the interactions between students like Debra and their peers. After the lesson, the language arts teacher, sensitized by Ms. Sheila's and her own observations of Debra's preference to work with peers rather than adults, reflects aloud, "It's surprising what she [Debra] can do, if she's given her independence!"

Ms. Andrea's Experience

CHIME Charter Elementary School in the Los Angeles, California, area embraces a whole-school approach to inclusion.

General and special education teachers collaborate with paraeducators and other support specialists to co-teach lessons for children with and without disabilities. When you meet Ms. Andrea, she has worked as a paraeducator in the school for over three years. As you watch her work, you see her support not only several students with disabilities but other students in a classroom co-taught by a general educator, a special educator, and a student teacher. Several learning stations are set up around the classroom. When asked about the decisions she makes during her work in the classroom, Ms. Andrea describes her work this year. "At the beginning of the year, we discussed at length how we were intending to increase each student's independence. The goal was to support them to see how they can do it on their own. Hopefully, when they are older, they can do it completely independently."

> This school-wide effort is featured in both a video and a DVD of co-teaching (Thousand, Villa, Nevin, & Harris, 2007) and differentiation of instruction practices (Villa, Thousand, Nevin, & Harris, 2008).

When asked about the progress or growth she has noticed in the children, Ms. Andrea responds, "Oh, I've seen tremendous growth in all of the students I've worked with. [*She shrugs.*] First day of school, they don't know you and you don't know them...then there's the process of getting to know them. [*She smiles.*] First they'll test you—like they'll run outside, you know, or not want to do their work. Then as they get to know you and what you expect, you are also getting to know them and realizing how you can best support them. It's been fabulous to watch. Now they can sit through the whole school day." [*She smiles again.*]

During the lesson, you see Ms. Andrea going to the computer to search for some materials from the Internet that might support the instruction of students who are at one of the learning centers. When asked whether that is fairly common in what she does every day, Ms. Andrea explains, "It happens throughout the day because we have the two teachers in the classroom at the same time. This allows me as the paraprofessional to go in search of extra materials to support the lesson at the time. Yeah! I do make an effort to make sure that every student, regardless of their needs, gets access to the knowledge and information that I have available (or can get for them) throughout the day!"

Ms. Andrea's supervising special educator reinforces that Ms. Andrea's support role is for all students in the classroom, not just students with

IEPs. The special educator elaborates on the philosophy of the school: "Our paraeducators are trained to work with all the children. They are trained to teach children to be part of the classroom life. They look for opportunities to provide support [*she leans in*] and then back off [*she leans back*]. An example of this occurred in today's lesson when the paraeducator realized, as did I, that no one in the class understood the term 'sand spit' (a key concept in the story the class was reading). Even though I tried to draw an image of a sand spit, it was clear the students did not understand what it is. So, when Andrea found the picture on the Internet and brought it over to me for me to show the group, it was evident right away that they could understand. This was something I had not anticipated would be a problem—that the students would have that much difficulty with that one word!"

Offering an important caution about how paraeducators support students, the general educator explains, "I think it's important that we not take away the students' independence. We don't want the paraeducators to be Velcroed to the students throughout the lessons. We want the paraeducators to give the students their space, to be able to maybe work with some peers or do it alone. It's about respecting choice. A lot of times the paraeducator will notice that the modifications we created just aren't working for the student! They realize it's too easy or it might be too challenging. So many times, they will tweak the modification so as to add support for the student."

■ A NATIONAL STUDY OF PARAEDUCATORS IN INCLUSIVE CLASSROOMS

Ms. Sheila's experience in an Albuquerque classroom and Ms. Andrea's experience in a Los Angeles–area classroom inspired one of the authors to launch a national study. Its purpose was to discover the nature of the changing roles of paraeducators working in inclusive classrooms that include students with disabilities, students who speak languages other than English, students who are at risk for school failure, and students from other culturally and ethnically diverse heritages (Malian & Nevin, 2008; Nevin, Gonzalez, et al.; Nevin, Malian, & Liston, 2008). In the first three months of the study, 120 paraeducators completed the survey, which had been posted on a national paraeducator Web site. Respondents were predominantly women (98%) working in elementary schools. They had, on average, seven years of experience; quite a number had a family member or friend with a disability.

Common Issues of Paraeducators in Inclusive Classrooms

Results of this national survey reinforce what other studies have identified as issues for paraeducators working in inclusive settings (e.g., Devechhi & Rouse, 2007; Doyle, 2002; Marks et al., 1999; Pickett & Gerlach, 1997; Riggs & Mueller, 2001; Rueda & Monzo, 2002). Namely, the top issues were (a) how to share opinions about the children with whom they work, (b) time for collaboration with teachers and supervisors, and (c) the need for more training. In fact, the majority of respondents indicated that paraeducators need more training.

Although the participants revealed frustrations, they also made suggestions for how to deal with the issues. One paraeducator suggested, "Take the lead from the regular teacher—be flexible. Always show respect, even if you do not agree." Another wrote, "A willingness to 'go with the flow' is essential." Over 10% of the paraeducators offered advice such as "Be sure you have a good working relationship with the supervising teacher and/or case manager."

Roles of Paraeducators in Inclusive Classrooms

Some of the roles reported by paraeducators reflected the roles described in Table 3.1. For example, many stated they worked with children and youths who needed behavioral support or social skills training. Others echoed the literature that shows paraeducators in inclusive classrooms who work as members of collaborative teams to deliver instruction in reading and math through various activities (e.g., learning centers, cooperative learning groups, and one-to-one interactions).

An emerging role that was noted by approximately 10% of the paraeducators was their responsibility to deliver researched best practices such as required in a Response to Intervention (RtI) approach. A paraeducator from Illinois wrote, "Our district uses RtI. We have used the 'six minute solution' in reading that is very effective. We have resources that push in and pull out as needed." Another paraeducator, from Rhode Island, noted, "I have coached children in language arts under the supervision of a reading teacher." Still another paraeducator, from Michigan, described her responsibilities in this way: "I document notes on each child seen daily to measure progress and give [the notes about] strategies [to the teacher]." Two paraeducators from Oregon wrote, "I use DIBELS to monitor progress [of all the students]." Note: A system to frequently measure literacy skills, DIBELS is an acronym for Dynamic Indicators of Basic Early Literacy Skills. For more information, refer to DIBELS official Web site: http://dibels. uoregon.edu/

Advice Paraeducators Offer

It is revealing and touching to read that, when asked about the most important part of their work in inclusive classrooms, most paraeducators identified something that related to the students themselves. Appreciation for students' unique characteristics, including their strengths, was one important aspect of their job, as suggested by the following verbatim comments.

- "Each child learns differently."
- "Each child has talents or strengths that you can help to surface in the classroom to help build their self-esteem."
- "Each student learns at a different rate of speed."

A majority of paraeducators identified that they focus on "helping their students to learn" as a critical part of their job. For example, a paraeducator from New Mexico wrote, "The most important part of the work

I do in inclusive classrooms is meeting the students' needs and working with their IEP goals." Listen to other paraeducators' voices regarding the important parts of their work in inclusive classrooms:

- "Always smile. Give students praise when warranted."
- "Know each student's capabilities."
- "Keep in mind that you are the advocate for your students and need to do all you can to ensure their success."
- "Be flexible! Instruction may change even after it has been planned to accommodate the child; nothing is set in stone in an inclusive classroom!"
- "You should never hover over one child or draw attention to him."
- "Know when to provide one-to-one instruction and when to use a support strategy."
- "Have high expectations!"
- "Know how to accommodate your student within the curriculum."
- "Be flexible and adaptable for the changes and remember why we are doing this—for the child who needs us."
- "Make sure the curriculum goals are met along with IEP goals."

In summary, when asked what other paraeducators should know about inclusive classrooms, paraeducators in this national study overwhelmingly wrote statements that could be placed into one of two categories. The first category, "Be Willing to Ask," includes advice to ask questions, read books, collaborate and communicate with others in order to learn strategies to help the children. The second category, "Be Flexible," includes advice that ranges from "be prepared to be busy" to "be prepared to work with some people who may not know exactly what to do with you."

Finally, paraeducators' appreciation for the job is captured by one paraeducator who wrote, "There is nothing better than seeing the kids succeed!" and another, from New Mexico, who wrote, "We are so lucky to be in an inclusive classroom (^_^)."

■ ADVICE FROM PARAEDUCATOR SCENARIOS

Ms. Hernandez: Elementary School Scenario

Recall Ms. Hernandez, our paraeducator who works with both the second- and third-grade teams to intensify instruction in reading and math at Chaparral Valley Elementary. Ms. Hernandez's school has committed and restructured to intervene early with students who are having difficulty and to differentiate instruction so all students have high-quality instruction that matches where they are in the curriculum. When asked what her advice would be for paraeducators and teachers, she quickly responds, "Be sure to carve out time to plan, talk, and look at student data." Ms. Hernandez notes that "we are lucky at Chaparral Valley as we have Wednesday afternoons on our shortened day, to devote to grade-level meetings about our students and their progress. Our principal is the one that pushed us to use our time this way and holds us accountable for keeping meeting minutes and using the data we collect to show that students are making progress. And, if they are not, we have tools such as our SODAS problem-solving strategy to use to brainstorm how we might rearrange our resources or change how we are teaching these students so they can get back on track."

Ms. Hernandez's second piece of advice has to do with inclusive practices and the positive effect it has on student behavior. In the previous year, she provided instruction primarily in a "pullout" approach in a resource room. She had one group of boys, all of whom had Behavior Support Plans and had routinely been grouped together for instruction. They had been an ongoing challenge to get focused and to manage. This year, they remained in the general education classroom during *differentiated literacy group time* and the rest of the day, and their troublesome behaviors seem to have disappeared. Observing this, Ms. Hernandez advises paraeducators and teachers to "give students a chance to make it in general education with peer and/or adult support and the level of instruction they need. Just assume that all kids just want to fit in and can hold it together if they can count on us to pinpoint just what they need to learn so they can shine rather than fail in front of their classmates."

Ms. Hernandez's last piece of advice is related to job satisfaction. She muses, "If you want a paraeducator to really give 100%, realize that they need to be shown they are a valued member of the community by being given the training and support they need to learn how to do the job and get better at it. I have been blessed with all of the ongoing modeling, training, and feedback I have received from the reading specialist and my special educator supervisor about specific reading interventions. You can't underestimate how feeling competent can lead to increased confidence and job satisfaction. I wouldn't trade working at Chaparral Valley for a job at another school, because I feel like I can really learn how to become a great teacher here."

Ms. Bartolo: Middle School Scenario

As you will recall, Ms. Bartolo had a variety of job responsibilities. She was assigned to work with two veteran English teachers, to work with a new science teacher, to assist a student in the learning center, and to provide clerical support in the special education office. Reflecting upon the just-completed first half of the year, Ms. Bartolo recognizes that she has acquired a fair number of skills and increased confidence.

When asked what are the most important lessons she has learned, she notes, "Teachers are people too, and some will always be more confident and welcoming of your support in their classroom than others will." Ms. Bartolo also says that she has learned that it is important to advocate for herself. She is proud of the fact that when no job description was forthcoming, she developed one and shared it with the educators, requesting their input and feedback. She also celebrates the fact that she asked for clarification and help when it was needed and was successful in advocating for changes to Bradley's program and her role in the learning center. Ms. Bartolo concludes by saying, "It's good to just take a deep breath and realize that it is a process and some days will be better than others."

Mr. Anderson: Secondary School Scenario

Mr. Anderson very much enjoys his work at the high school and with the team of 10th-grade general and special educators with whom he has worked for four years. Recall that Mr. Anderson is attending school and earning his teaching credential—he believes that serving as a paraeducator and having the opportunity to work in a variety of classrooms with a variety of teachers has been more valuable to his teacher preparation than any course he has taken at the university. Mr. Anderson feels that he has been able to learn firsthand an array of instructional and classroom management strategies that he will use when he has his own classroom. He also notes, "I intend to be grateful and welcoming when a paraeducator is assigned to my classroom. I know the powerful contribution that paraeducators can make to student and teacher success!"

■ SUMMARY

Now that you have nearly completed reading this final chapter, what advice might you offer paraeducators regarding their roles in co-taught classrooms? Whether you are a teacher or a paraeducator, do you have new insights on working with one another? Do you have some new actions that you might offer if you have the chance to work as or with a paraeducator in a co-taught classroom?

Do you have some new ideas about how to resolve issues that arise when working with a variety of teachers? In the scenarios described throughout the book, we guided you through the process of understanding the variety of work situations that paraeducators commonly face. We illustrated through the scenarios that resolving issues is a developmental process that requires respect for individual differences, support to learn and practice new skills, and appropriate supervision and professional development of all involved. For example, some paraeducators enter their work environments with structured job descriptions; others, like Ms. Bartolo (the middle school paraeducator), have no clear job description. Ms. Bartolo was also paired with a first-year teacher, Mr. Ruhan, who was reluctant to work with another adult in his classroom. Do you remember the process by which Ms. Bartolo was able to successfully address these issues and improve her working conditions and outlook? Ms. Bartolo engaged in structured collaborative planning sessions with the two experienced teachers with whom she worked, Ms. Cole and Ms. Hendrickson, who also coached her to draft a job description. They worked with her to complete the Co-Teacher Roles and Responsibilities Matrix (see Resource A or Table 3.5). These two experienced co-teachers helped Ms. Bartolo become an independent learner who engaged in online learning to become a self-advocate. With the help of Ms. Bartolo's special education supervisor, Mr. Ruhan slowly began to change the way he interacted with Ms. Bartolo in his classroom. Ms. Bartolo then was able to take on more of a complementary co-teaching role that allowed Mr. Ruhan to circulate among the students, and he began to feel that Ms. Bartolo's presence was more of an asset than a burden.

Ms. Bartolo was further coached and supervised to learn the parallel co-teaching approach where she became independently capable of supervising a learning center. In Mr. Ruhan's classroom, her role evolved into using the supportive as well as the complementary co-teaching approach. In summary, her advice in this chapter becomes all the more poignant: "Teachers are people too, and some will always be more confident and welcoming of your support in their classroom than others will." She also mentioned how important it is to become a self-advocate.

Tolerance for and valuing of the individual differences of teachers is an important component of successful work in inclusive schools. Tolerance for and valuing of the individual differences of the children and youths who attend our schools is equally important. We end by reflecting on the wisdom of Kent Gerlach, who instructs us that "our task is to teach the kids we have, not the kinds of kids we used to have, want to have, or the kids that exist in our dreams" (personal communication, April 17, 2008). Our fervent hope is that you are inspired by this quote as well as what you have read in this book to collaborate to craft the most effective instruction for *all* students.

We are intensely aware that, in today's schools, there are barriers to having paraeducators meaningfully involved in the process of collaborative planning and teaching. And we know that the intellectually and interpersonally demanding efforts to meet and overcome these barriers are worth the potential positive outcomes for the kids and those who teach them. After all, paraeducators are here to teach and benefit the kids—the only kids we have!

Resources

■   **RESOURCE A**

Co-Teaching Roles and Responsibilities Matrix

CODE KEY

P = Primary Responsibility; S = Secondary Responsibility; E = Equal Responsibility; I = Input

Responsibility	Name:	Name:	Name:	Name:
Develop units, projects, lessons				
Instruct students				
Monitor student progress				
Assign grades				
Create advance organizers				
Note-taking, model use of graphic organizers				
Facilitate peer support, friendship				
Discipline/behavior management				
Communicate with parents				
Develop Individual Education Programs (IEPs)				
Communicate with administrators				
Attend team meetings				
Train paraeducator				
Supervise paraeducator				
Other				
Other				

RESOURCE B ■

Template for Gathering Information About Student Characteristics and Classroom Demands

Student Characteristics	Classroom Demands
Strengths Background Knowledge and Experiences Interests Learning Style(s) Multiple Intelligences Important Relationships Other: _____ Other: _____	**Content Demands** How is the content made available to the learners? What multi-level materials are used?
	Process Demands What processes or instructional methods do the co-teachers use to facilitate student learning?
Goals Does this learner have any unique goals related to academic learning, communication, English language acquisition, and/or social-emotional functioning? Are there particular concerns about this learner?	**Product Demands** How do the students demonstrate what they have learned? How are students assessed or graded?

■ RESOURCE C

A Checklist of Sample Supplemental Supports, Aids, and Services

Directions: When co-teachers consider the need for personalized supports, aids, or services for a student, use this checklist to help identify which supports will be the least intrusive, only as special as necessary, and the most natural to the context of the classroom.

Environmental

_____ Preferential seating

_____ Planned seating

       _____ Bus _____ Classroom _____ Lunchroom _____ Auditorium _____ Other

_____ Alter physical room arrangement (Specify: _____)

_____ Use study carrels or quiet areas

_____ Define area concretely (e.g., carpet squares, tape on floor, rug area)

_____ Reduce/minimize distractions

       _____ Visual _____ Spatial _____ Auditory _____ Movement

_____ Teach positive rules for use of space

Pacing of Instruction

_____ Extend time requirements _____ Vary activity often _____ Allow breaks

_____ Omit assignments requiring copying in timed situations

_____ Additional copy of the text sent home for summer preview

_____ Home set of materials for preview or review

Presentation of Subject Matter

_____ Teach to the student's learning style/strength intelligences

       _____ Verbal/Linguistic   _____ Math/Logical   _____ Visual/Spatial

       _____ Naturalist   _____ Bodily/Kinesthetic   _____ Musical

       _____ Interpersonal   _____ Intrapersonal

_____ Use active, experiential learning

_____ Use specialized curriculum

_____ Tape class lectures and discussions to replay later

_____ Use American Sign Language and/or total communication

_____ Provide prewritten notes, outline, or organizer (e.g., mind map)

_____ Copy of classmate's notes (e.g., use NCR paper, photocopy)

_____ Functional and meaningful application of academic skills

_____ Present demonstrates and models

Presentation of Subject Matter

_____ Use manipulatives in mathematics and real objects

_____ Highlight critical information or main ideas

_____ Pre-teach vocabulary

_____ Make and use vocabulary files or provide vocabulary lists

_____ Reduce the language level of the reading assignment

_____ Use facilitated communication

_____ Use visual organizers/sequences

_____ Use paired reading/writing

_____ Reduce seat time in class or activities

_____ Use diaries or learning logs

_____ Reword, rephrase instructions, questions

_____ Preview and review major concepts in primary language

Materials

_____ Limit amount of material on a page

_____ Audiotape texts and other class materials

_____ Use study guides and advanced organizers

_____ Use supplementary materials

_____ Provide note-taking assistance

_____ Copy class notes

_____ Scan tests and class notes into computer

_____ Large print   _____ Braille material

_____ Use communication book or board

_____ Provide assistive technology and software (e.g., Intelli-Talk)

Specialized Equipment or Procedure

_____ Wheelchair   _____ Walker

_____ Standing Board   _____ Positioning

_____ Computer   _____ Computer Software

_____ Electronic typewriter _____ Video

_____ Modified keyboard   _____ Voice synthesize

_____ Switches   _____ Augmentative communication devise

_____ Catheterization   _____ Suctioning

_____ Restroom equipment   _____ Braces

_____ Customized mealtime utensils, plates, cups, and other materials

(_Continued_)

(Continued)

Assignment Modification

_____ Give directions in small, distinct steps (written/picture/verbal)

_____ Use written backup for oral directions

_____ Use pictures as supplement to oral directions

_____ Lower difficulty level   _____ Raise difficulty level

_____ Shorten assignments   _____ Reduce paper and pencil tasks

_____ Read or tape record directions to the student(s)

_____ Give extra cues or prompts

_____ Allow student to record or type assignment

_____ Adapt worksheets and packets

_____ Use compensatory procedures by providing alternate assignment, when demands of class conflict with student capabilities

_____ Ignore spelling errors/sloppy work _____ Ignore penmanship

_____ Develop alternative rubrics

Self-Management/Follow-Through

_____ Provide pictorial or word daily or weekly schedule

_____ Provide student calendars

_____ Check often for understanding/review

_____ Request parent reinforcement

_____ Have student repeat directions

_____ Teach study skills

_____ Use binders to organize material

_____ Design/write/use long-term assignments timelines

_____ Review and practice in real situations

_____ Plan for generalization by teaching skill in several environments

Testing Adaptations

_____ Provide oral instructions and/or read test questions

_____ Use pictorial instructions/questions

_____ Read test to student

_____ Preview language of test questions

_____ Ask questions that have applications in real setting

_____ Individualized administration of test

_____ Use short answer _____ Use multiple-choice _____ Shorten length

_____ Extend time frame _____ Use open-note/open-book tests

_____ Modify format to reduce visual complexity or confusion

Social Interaction Support

_____ Use natural peer supports and multiple, rotating peers

_____ Use peer advocacy

_____ Use cooperative group learning

_____ Institute peer tutoring

_____ Structure opportunities for social interaction (e.g., Circle of Friends)

_____ Focus on social process rather than the end product

_____ Structure shared experiences in school and extracurricular activities

_____ Teach friendship, sharing, negotiation skills to classmates

_____ Teach social communication skills

       _____ Greetings _____ Conversation _____ Turn Taking _____ Sharing

       _____ Negotiation Other: _____ Other: _____

Level of Staff Support (Consider after considering previous categories)

_____ Consultation

_____ Stop-in support (one to three times per week)

_____ Part-time daily support

_____ Co-teaching (parallel, supportive, complementary, or team-teaching)

_____ Daily in-class staff support

_____ Total staff support (staff are in close proximity)

_____ One-on-one assistant

_____ Specialized personnel support (If indicated, identify time needed)

Support	Time Needed
_____ Instructional Support Assistant	_____
_____ Health Care Assistant	_____
_____ Behavior Assistant	_____
_____ Signing Assistant	_____
_____ Nursing	_____
_____ Occupational Therapy	_____
_____ Physical Therapy	_____
_____ Speech and Language Therapist	_____
_____ Augmentative Communication Specialist	_____
_____ Transportation	_____
_____ Counseling	_____
_____ Adaptive Physical Education	_____
_____ Transition Planning	_____
_____ Orientation/Mobility	_____
_____ Career Counseling	_____

■ **RESOURCE D**

Team Summary: Our Likes and Dislikes When Working With Others

Directions: Indicate which of the listed actions/behaviors you enjoy engaging in when working with others on a team.

When all team members have indicated their preferences, discuss your team's summary profile. What are the strengths of team members? Given these preferences and skills, what issue or challenges should be easy or exciting for your team to address? What kinds of problems might you anticipate among team members?

Collaborative Behaviors During and Following Meetings	Member Name:	Member Name:	Member Name:	Member Name:	Member Name:
Serving as a recorder					
Serving as a timekeeper					
Sharing information					
Asking for help					
Asking questions					
Encouraging participation					
Being a process observer					
Sharing feelings					
Dealing with conflict					
Assuming leadership					
Following an agenda					
Analyzing problems					
Accepting criticism of my ideas					
Weighing pros and cons of options before making decisions					
Brainstorming					
Listening to people describe their feelings					

Collaborative Behaviors During and Following Meetings	Member Name:	Member Name:	Member Name:	Member Name:	Member Name:
Compromising					
Summarizing					
Delegating tasks to someone else					
Changing the way I do things					
Being diplomatic					
Speaking					
Listening					
Goal setting					
Meeting deadlines					
Giving others recognition and credit					
Doing research					
Data collection					
Other: _____					

ACTION PLAN:

How will you deal proactively with future conflicts or disagreements?

_____

_____

What training opportunities might team members arrange or take advantage of to increase your team members' collaborative skills?

_____

_____

Are there any other individuals with complementary skills that you might want to add to your team?

_____

■ **RESOURCE E**

Collaborative Planning Meeting Agenda

People present: _____   _____

_____   _____   _____

_____   _____   _____

Absentees: _____   _____

_____   _____   _____

Others who need to know: _____   _____

Roles	This meeting	Next meeting
Timekeeper	_____	_____
Recorder	_____	_____
Summarizer/Checker	_____	_____
Encourager/Praiser	_____	_____
Jargon Buster	_____	_____
Other(s):	_____	_____

AGENDA

Agenda Items	Time limit
1. Review agenda and positive comments	_____
2.	_____
3.	_____
4. Pause for group processing of progress toward task accomplishment and use of interpersonal skills	_____
5.	_____
6.	_____
7. Final group processing of task and relationship	_____

MINUTES OF OUTCOMES

Action items	Person(s) responsible	By when?
1. Communicate outcomes to absent members and others		
2.		
3.		

AGENDA BUILDING FOR NEXT MEETING

Date: _____   **Time:** _____   **Location:** _____

Expected agenda items

1.

2.

RESOURCE F ■

Checklist: Are We Really a Collaborative Team?

Directions: For a team score, mark a check under Yes or No for each of the 20 statements.

Yes	No	In our collaborative planning meetings:
		Face-to-Face Interactions
		1. Do we meet in a comfortable environment?
		2. Do we arrange ourselves in a circle so we can hear each other and see each other's facial expressions?
		3. Is our group size manageable (6 or fewer members)?
		4. Do we meet regularly at times and locations agreed upon in advance by teammates?
		5. Do we use a structured agenda with time limits for agenda items agreed upon at the previous meeting?
		6. Do needed members receive a timely invitation? (Note: Needed members may change from meeting to meeting, based upon agenda items.)
		7. Do we start and end on time?
		8. Do we update tardy members at a break or after the meeting rather than stopping the meeting midstream?
		Positive Interdependence
		9. Have we publicly discussed and agreed upon the group's overall goals, purposes, and responsibilities?
		10. Do we distribute leadership by rotating roles (e.g., recorder, timekeeper, encourager, agreement checker)?
		11. Do we start each meeting with positive comments and devote time to celebrating successes?
		12. Do we have fun at our meetings?
		Social Skills
		13. Have we established a set of group ground rules or norms and committed to abiding by these norms?
		14. Do we explain the group's norms to new members?
		15. Do we create an atmosphere for safely expressing genuine perspectives (negative and positive)?
		16. Do we acknowledge and deal with conflict during meetings?
		17. Do we have a communication system for absent members and people who are not regular team members but who need to know about our decisions (e.g., administrators)?
		18. Do we agree on the process for making a particular decision (e.g., majority vote, consensus, unanimous decision)?
		Group Processing
		19. Do we build in time at the end of each meeting to reflect upon and set goals for improving our interactions during meetings?
		20. Do we study about or arrange for training to improve targeted social skills (e.g., conflict resolution or mediation)?
		TOTAL (Out of maximum of 20 items × number of team members)

■ RESOURCE G

A SODAS Template for Problem Solving

SITUATION (Define the problem):

_____

_____

OPTIONS:

1. _____ 2. _____ 3._____

DISADVANTAGES:

a. _____ a. _____ a. _____

b. _____ b. _____ b. _____

c. _____ c _____ c. _____

d. _____ d. _____ d. _____

ADVANTAGES:

a. _____ a. _____ a. _____

b. _____ b. _____ b. _____

d. _____ d. _____ d. _____

d. _____ d. _____ d. _____

SOLUTION:

If you agree to a solution, *make a plan.*

(Who will do what, when? How you know whether the plan is working?)

Template for a Co-Teaching Daily Lesson Plan

Date: _____ **Co-Teachers:** _____

Content Area(s): _____ _____

(Names)

Lesson Objectives:

Content Standards Addressed:

Underline the Co-Teaching Approach(es) Used:

Supportive   Parallel   Complementary   Team Teaching

What is the room arrangement? Will other spaces outside of the classroom be used? (Draw a picture of the room arrangement.)

What materials do the co-teachers need?

How is student learning assessed by co-teachers?

What specific supports, aids, or services do select students need? (See Resource C for suggestions.)

What does each co-teacher do before, during, and after the lesson?

Co-Teacher Name:		
What are the specific tasks that I do BEFORE the lesson?		
What are the specific tasks that I do DURING the lesson?		
What are the specific tasks that I do AFTER the lesson?		

Where, when, and how do co-teachers debrief and evaluate the outcomes of the lesson?

RESOURCE I   ■

Professional Development Opportunities— Materials and Web Sites

Professional Development Materials

Bueno Center for Multicultural Education. (1997). *7 Modules for Para-Educators in Culturally & Linguistically Diverse Classrooms.* Boulder, CO: University of Colorado, Bilingual Special Education Training of Trainers Institute.

Fenn, K. (2005). *Basic facilitation for paraprofessionals: Color me successful—Ideas to grow by for beginning and experienced paraprofessionals.* Hartford, CT: SERC. Retrieved April 27, 2008, from http://paraconnect.com/ColorMeSuccessful.html

Fenn, K., & White, I. (2007, May). *Paraprofessionals as partners initiative for job embedded professional development study groups.* Paper presented at National Paraprofessional Resource Center Annual Conference, Albuquerque, NM.

Lachina, K., & Brogdon, T. (2000). *Ten tips for paraeducators: Classroom aides support for teaching, fostering student independence, and discouraging learned helplessness.* A collaborative publication from the Pennsylvania Department of Education, Bureau of Special Education, Pennsylvania Training and Technical Assistance Network, and Pennsylvania Partnership for Professional Development.

Morgan, R., Forbush, D., & Avis, D. (2001). *Enhancing skills of para-educators: A video-assisted program, 2nd ed.* (ESP 2). Logan: Utah State University, Technology, Research, & Instruction in Special Education.

Rueda, R., & Monzo, P. (2002). Apprenticeship for teaching: Professional development issues surrounding the collaborative relationship between teachers and paraeducators. *Teaching and Teacher Education, 18*(5), 503–521.

Thousand, J. S., Villa, R. A., & Nevin, A. I. (2007). *Differentiating instruction: Collaborative planning and teaching for universally designed learning: A multimedia kit for professional development.* Thousand Oaks, CA: Corwin Press.

Villa, R. A., Thousand, J. S., & Nevin, A. I. (2008a). *A guide to co-teaching: Practical tips for facilitating student learning, 2nd edition: A multimedia kit for professional development.* Thousand Oaks, CA: Corwin Press.

Villa, R. A., Thousand, J. S., & Nevin, A. I. (2008b). *Co-teaching at-a-glance* [laminated reference guide]. Port Chester, NY: National Professional Resources.

Professional Development Web Sites

- National Resource Center for Paraprofessionals (NRCP)
  http://www.nrcpara.org/
  Marilyn Likens and Teri Wallace maintain this richly resourceful project to improve the recruitment, deployment, supervision, and career development of paraprofessionals.

- The National Clearinghouse for Paraprofessional Pathways Into Teaching http://www.usc.edu/dept/education/CMMR/Clearinghouse.html
  This Web site is frequently updated to provide multiple resources, training programs, and research articles.
- The PAR²A Center in Colorado
  http://www.paracenter.org/PARACenter/misc/links.aspx
  Nancy French maintains this superb resource for training and references to articles and books for paraeducator employment, training, and supervision.
- Ashbaker, B., & Morgan, J. *Maximizing assistance: Supervising paraeducators in your classrooms.* NY: Pearson. Association for Supervision and Curriculum Development (ASCD) offers online training for teachers and administrators through access to http://pdonline.ascd.org/pd_online/new.
- The Northwest Regional Laboratory
  http://www.nwrac.org/para/guide/resources.html
  This Web site hosts the regularly updated *Oregon Resource Guide to Paraeducator Issues.*
- U. S. Department of Education (USDOE)
  http://www.ed.gov/pubs/Paraprofessionals/index.html
  Maintains an up-to-date overview of issues and policies related to paraprofessionals.

Glossary

Active Learning—This term refers to anything that involves students in doing things and thinking about the things they are doing. Active learning might include a spectrum of activities, from a modified lecture format to role-playing, simulation, games, project work, cooperative problem solving, collaborative research, partner learning, service learning, and teaching others.

Collaboration—Collaboration is a process where people "work jointly with others especially in an intellectual endeavor" (Merriam-Webster: http://www.merriam-webster.com/dictionary/collaborate). In the context of this book, teachers, paraeducators, and others collaborate to increase the effectiveness of instruction for students in diverse classrooms.

Cooperative Process—The cooperative process is an essential element of successful co-teaching and includes face-to-face interaction, positive interdependence, interpersonal skills, monitoring the progress of the co-teachers, and individual accountability.

Co-Teaching—Co-teaching is two or more people sharing responsibility for teaching.

Council for Exceptional Children (CEC) Standards for Paraprofessionals—The CEC standards describe knowledge and skills for paraprofessionals who work with children with disabilities. Three examples follow:

- Standard 3: Know the rights and responsibilities of families and children as they relate to individuals.
- Standard 9: Demonstrate sensitivity to the diversity of individuals and families.
- Standard 10: Collaboration: Knowledge of common concerns of families of individuals with exceptional learning needs.

DI—DI is an acronym for *differentiated instruction*, which is defined as a way for teachers to recognize and react responsively to their students' varying background knowledge, readiness, languages, learning preferences, and interests (Hall, 2002).

ELL—ELL is an acronym for *English language learner*. Teachers of English language learners assist these students through in-classroom support or resource room support. Instruction of English language learners is sometimes referred to as "English as a foreign language (EFL)" or "English for speakers of other languages (ESOL)."

Highly Qualified Paraprofessionals—The No Child Left Behind Act of 2001 requires paraeducators to be highly qualified in order to work in schools. The act articulates specific requirements paraeducators must meet, including having at least two years or 48 semester units of postsecondary education *or* a high school diploma plus a pass score on a formal state assessment or a local, state-approved assessment of academic skills.

IDEIA—IDEIA is an acronym for the Individuals with Disabilities Education Improvement Act, the 2004 reauthorization of the federal legislation that guarantees students with disabilities a free and appropriate education in the least restrictive environment. This latest reauthorization emphasizes the importance of students with disabilities having access to the core general education curriculum through highly qualified teachers and providing early learning support for struggling learners through a Response to Intervention approach.

Inclusive Education—Inclusive education is a process where schools welcome, value, support, and empower all students in shared environments and experiences for the purpose of attaining the goals of education.

Monitoring—Monitoring student progress toward learning goals occurs on a regular basis. Paraprofessionals can be assigned the task of evaluating student work and then entering students' grades on daily assignments and homework in the teacher's grade book. Other methods include IEP Monitoring, ABC Sheets, Classroom Observation, Frequency Charts, Social Skills Monitoring, and Informal Inventories.

NCLB—NCLB is the acronym for the No Child Left Behind Act of 2001 (Pub. L. No. 107–110), a federal mandate for ensuring that schools and teachers are accountable for the academic progress of all students in public schools.

Paraeducator—A paraeducator is a school employee who "provides instructional, safety, and/or therapeutic services to students" (French, 2008a, p. 1). Paraeducators work under the supervision of a professional in a position that might have one of the following titles: teaching assistant, paraprofessional, aide, instructional aide, health care aide, educational technician, literacy or math tutor, job coach, instructional assistant, or educational assistant. The two most frequently used terms for describing a person in this role are *paraprofessional* and *paraeducator*.

RtI—RtI is an acronym for Response to Intervention, which allows professional educators to design and evaluate academic and behavioral interventions for students at increasing levels of intensity depending on the students' reactions to the intervention. RtI features the following elements: (1) high-quality classroom instruction, (2) research-based instruction, (3) classroom performance measures, (4) universal screening, (5) continuous progress monitoring, (6) research-based interventions, (7) progress monitoring during interventions, and (8) fidelity measures (Graner, Faggella-Luby, & Fritschmann, 2005).

Stages of Co-Teacher Development—Similar to the stages of group development, co-teachers should expect to experience and need different communication skills depending on whether they are just beginning (forming), deciding on how they'll work together (functioning), working through the problems they might face (formulating), or managing conflicts of ideas or procedures about what to emphasize or how to teach certain students (fermenting). The social interaction and communication skills they use at each of these stages will facilitate the development of their cohesiveness as a co-teaching team (Villa, Thousand, & Nevin, 2008a).

References

Anderson, L., & Krathwohl, D. (Eds.). (2001). *A taxonomy for learning, teaching, and assessing: A revision of Bloom's taxonomy of educational objectives.* New York: Longman.

Armstrong, T. (2000). *Multiple intelligences in the classroom* (2nd ed.). Alexandria, VA: Association for Supervision and Curriculum Development.

Ashbaker, B., & Morgan, J. (2000). Bilingual paraeducators: What we can learn from Rosa. *National Association of Secondary School Principals Bulletin (NASSP), 84*(614), 53–56.

Ashbaker, B., & Morgan, J. (2001). Paraeducators: A powerful human resource. *Streamlined Seminar, 19*(2), 1–4. Quarterly newsletter of the National Association of Elementary School Principals.

Ashbaker, B., & Morgan, J. (2005). *Paraprofessionals in the classroom.* Boston: Allyn & Bacon.

Batsche, G. (2006). *Response to intervention: Policy considerations and implementation.* Alexandria, VA: National Association of State Directors of Special Education (NASDSE), Inc.

Bloom, B. S., Englehart, M. B., Furst, E. J., Hill, W. H., & Krathwohl, D. R. (1956). *Taxonomy of Educational Objectives, the classification of educational goals – Handbook I: Cognitive Domain.* New York: McKay.

Burgstahler, S., Duclos, R., & Turcotte, M. (1999). *Preliminary findings: Faculty, teaching assistant, and student perceptions regarding accommodating students with disabilities in postsecondary environments.* Seattle, WA: University of Washington, Disabilities-Opportunities-Internetworking-Technology (DO-IT) Retrieved May 5, 2008, from http://www.washington.edu/doit/TeamN/profession.html

Council for Exceptional Children (CEC). (2003). *What every special educator must know: CEC International Standards for Entry into Professional Practice*, 5th ed., Arlington, VA: Author. Retrieved May 5, 2008, http://www.cec.sped.org/Content/NavigationMenu/ProfessionalDevelopment/ProfessionalStandards/Red_book_5th_edition.pdf

Devechhi, C., & Rouse, M. (2007, April). *What is "special" about teachers and teaching assistants' collaboration? An ethnographic exploration of teachers and teaching assistants supporting each other in secondary schools.* Paper presented at annual conference of the American Educational Research Association, Chicago.

Downing, J., Ryndak, D., & Clark, D. (2000). Paraeducators in inclusive classrooms. *Remedial and Special Education, 21*, 171–181.

Doyle, M. B. (2002). *The paraprofessional's guide to inclusive education: Working as a team* (2nd ed.). Baltimore: Paul H. Brookes.

Etscheidt, S. (2005). Paraprofessional services for students with disabilities: A legal analysis of issues. *Research and Practice for Persons with Severe Disabilities, 30*, 60–80.

Fenn, K. (2005). *Basic facilitation for paraprofessionals: Color me successful— Ideas to grow by for beginning and experienced paraprofessionals.* Hartford, CT: SERC. Retrieved April 27, 2008, from http://paraconnect.com/ColorMeSuccessful.html

Fenn, K., & White, I. (2007, May). *Paraprofessionals as partners initiative for job embedded professional development study groups.* Paper presented at National Paraprofessional Resource Center Annual Conference, Albuquerque, NM.

French, N. (1999). Topic #2: Paraeducators and teachers: Shifting roles. *Teaching Exceptional Children 32 (2),* 69–73.

French, N. (2001). Supervising paraprofessionals: A survey of teacher practices. *The Journal of Special Education, 35*(1), 41–53.

French, N. (2002). *Managing paraeducators in your school: How to hire, train, and supervise non-certified staff.* Thousand Oaks, CA: Corwin Press.

French, N. (2003). Management of paraeducators. In A. Pickett & K. Gerlach (Eds.) *Supervising para-educators in school settings: A team approach* (2nd ed). Austin, TX: PRO-ED Publishers.

French, N. (2007). *Paraeducator's resource guide,* [laminated reference guide]. Port Chester, NY: National Professional Resources, Inc.

French, N. (2008a). *A guide to the supervision of paraeducators.* Port Chester, NY: National Professional Resources, Inc.

French, N. (2008b). *A paraeducator's resource guide* [laminated reference guide]. Port Chester, NY: National Professional Resources, Inc.

French, N., & Chopra, R. (1999). Parent perspectives on the roles of paraprofessionals in inclusive classrooms. *The Journal of the Association of Persons with Severe Handicaps, 24*(4), 259–272.

Gardner, H. (1999). *Intelligence reframed: Multiple intelligences for the 21st century.* New York: Basic Books.

Gehrke, R., & Murri, N. (2006). Beginning special educators' intent to stay in special education: Why they like it here. *Teacher Education and Special Education, 29*(3), 179–190.

Gerlach, K. (2006). *Let's team up: A checklist for paraeducators, teachers, and principals (4th printing).* Washington, DC: National Education Association.

Giangreco, M., Broer, S., & Edelman, S. (2002). Schoolwide planning to improve paraeducator supports: A pilot study. *Rural Special Education Quarterly, 21*(1), 3–15.

Giangreco, M., Smith, C., & Pinckney, E. (2006). Addressing the paraprofessional dilemma in an inclusive classroom: A program description. *Research & Practice for Persons with Severe Disabilities, 31*(3), 215–229.

Giangreco, M., Yuan, S., McKenzie, B., Cameron, P., & Flalka, J. (2005). Be careful what you wish for...Five reasons to be concerned about the assignment of individual paraprofessionals. *Exceptional Children, 37*(5), 28–34.

Glasser, W. (1999). *Choice theory: A new psychology of personal freedom.* New York: Perennial.

Grady, M. (Ed.). (2007). Collaboration makes a difference. *The Special Edge, 19*(3), 6–7, 9, 11.

Graner, P., Faggella-Luby, M., & Fritschmann, N. (2005). An overview of responsiveness to intervention: What practitioners ought to know. *Topics in Language Disorders, 25(2)*, 93–105.

Hall, T. (2002). *Differentiated instruction*. CAST: National Center on Accessing the General Curriculum: Effective classroom practices report. Retrieved May 5, 2008, from http://www.cast.org/publications/ncac/ncac_diffinstruc.html

Hazel, J., Schumaker, J., Sherman, J., & Sheldon, J. (1995). *ASSET: A social skills program for adolescents*. Champaign, IL: Research Press.

Hourcade, J., & Bauwens, J. (2002). *Cooperative teaching: Re-building and sharing the schoolhouse*. Austin, TX: PRO-ED.

Idol, L., Nevin, A., & Paolucci-Whitcomb, P. (2000). *Collaborative consultation* (3rd ed.). Austin, TX: PRO-ED.

Individuals with Disabilities Educational Improvement Act (IDEIA). (2004). Public Law 108–446, 20 USC 1401.

Johnson, D. W., & Johnson, F. F. (1997). *Joining together: Group theory and skills* (6th ed). Needham Heights, MA: Allyn & Bacon.

Koroloff, N. (1996). Linking low-income families to children's mental health services: An outcome study. *Journal of Emotional and Behavioral Disorders, 4*(1), 2–11.

Malian, I., & Nevin, A. (2008, January). *Paraeducators in inclusive classrooms: A national survey*. Paper presented at the Hawaii International Higher Education Conference, Honolulu.

Marks, S., Schrader, C., & Levine, M. (1999). Para-educator experiences in inclusive classrooms: Helping, hovering, or holding their own? *Exceptional Children, 65*(3), 315–328.

Marzano, M., Pickering, D., & Pollack, J. (2001). *Classroom instruction that works: Research-based strategies for increasing student achievement*. Alexandria, VA: Association for Supervision and Curriculum Development.

Morgan, R., Forbush, D., & Avis, D. (2001). *Enhancing skills of para-educators: A video-assisted program, 2nd ed.* (ESP 2). Logan: Utah State University, TRI-SPED.

Mueller, P. (2002). The paraeducator paradox. *Exceptional Parent, 32*(9), 64–67.

Mueller, P., & Murphy, F. (2001). Determining when a student requires paraeducator support. *Teaching Exceptional Children, 33*(6), 22–27.

National Center for Education Statistics (NCES). (2000). *Education statistics: Elementary and secondary schools and staffing survey: Non-professional Staff in the Schools and Staffing Survey (SASS) and Common Core of Data (CCD, Working Paper No. 2000-13*. Washington, DC: US Department of Education, Office of Education Research.

National Center on Educational Restructuring and Inclusion. (1995). *National study on inclusion: Overview and summary report*. City University of New York, Graduate School and University Center.

Nevin, A., Cramer, E., & Salazar, L. , & Voigt, J. (2007, April). *Instructional modifications, adaptations, and accommodations of co-teachers who loop: A case study*. Paper presented at American Educational Research Association, Special Education Research Special Interest Group, Chicago.

Nevin, A., Gonzalez, L., Marshall, D., Moores-Abdool, W., Salazar, M., Voigt, J., (2007, May). *A peek into role changes and demands: What do para-educators DO in inclusive classrooms?* Paper presented at the 2007 Annual Conference for Paraprofessionals and Related Service Providers: Ensuring Student Success—Teams that Work. National Resource Center for Paraprofessionals, Albuquerque, NM ERIC Document #ED499806

Nevin, A., Malian, I., & Liston, A. (2008, April). *Paraeducator's profile in inclusive classrooms: Analysis of national survey data and follow-up case study interviews in California.* Paper presented at the 27th Annual Conference for Paraprofessionals and Related Service Providers, Hartford, CT. ERIC Document #ED501238

No Child Left Behind Act (NCLB). (2001). Public Law No. 107–110.

Palmer, D., Borthwick-Duffy, S., Widaman, K., & Best, S. (1998). Influences on parent perceptions of inclusive practices for their children with mental retardation. *American Journal on Mental Retardation, 3,* 272–287.

The PAR²A Center Policy and Research Special Interest Group. (2005, August). *Skill Standards for Paraeducators in Colorado.* Retrieved May 5, 2008, from www .paracenter.org/PARACenter/library

Perez, J., & Murdock, J. (1999). *Investigating the effects of a paraprofessional teaching sharing behaviors to young children with special needs in an inclusive kindergarten classroom.* Dissertation. University of New Orleans.

Pickett, A. L. (2002). Paraeducators: The evolution in their roles, responsibilities, training, and supervision. *IMPACT, 15*(2), 2–3. Retrieved May 5, 2008, from http://www.ici.umn.edu/products/impact/152/default.html

Pickett, A. L., & Gerlach, K. (Eds.). (1997). *Supervising para-educators in school settings: A team approach.* Austin, TX: PRO-ED.

Pickett, A. L., & Gerlach, K. (Eds.). (2003). *Supervising para-educators in school settings: A team approach, 2nd ed.* Austin, TX: PRO-ED.

Piletic, C., Davis, R., & Aschemeier, A. (2005). Paraeducators in physical education. *Journal of Physical Education Recreation and Dance, 76*(5), 47–55.

Radaszewski-Byrne, M. (1997). Issues in the development of guidelines for the preparation and use of speech-language paraprofessionals and their speech-language supervisors working in education settings. *Journal of Children's Communication Development, 18*(1), 5–21.

Riggs, C., & Mueller, P. (2001). Employment and utilization of paraeducators in inclusive settings. *Journal of Special Education, 35*(1), 54–62.

Rogan, P., & Held, M. (1999). Paraprofessionals in job coach roles. *The Journal of the Association for Persons with Severe Handicaps, 19,* 32–42.

Rueda, R., & Monzo, P. (2002). Apprenticeship for teaching: Professional development issues surrounding the collaborative relationship between teachers and para-educators. *Teaching and Teacher Education, 18*(5), 503–521.

Skär, L., & Tam, M. (2001). My assistant and I: Disabled children's and adolescents' roles and relationships to their assistants. *Disability & Society, 16*(7), 917–931.

Thousand, J., & Villa, R. (2000). Collaborative teaming: A powerful tool in school restructuring. In R. A. Villa & J. S. Thousand. *Restructuring for caring and effec-*

tive instruction: Piecing the puzzle together (2nd ed., pp. 254–293). Baltimore: Paul H. Brookes Publishing Co.

Thousand, J., Villa, R., & Nevin, A. (2007). *Differentiating instruction: Collaborative planning and teaching for universally designed learning.* Thousand Oaks, CA: Corwin Press.

Thousand, J., Villa, R., Nevin, A., & Paolucci-Whitcomb, P. (1995). A rationale and vision for collaborative consultation. In W. Stainback & S. Stainback (Eds.), *Controversial issues confronting special education: Divergent perspectives* (2nd ed., pp. 223–232). Baltimore: Paul H. Brookes Publishing Co.

Thousand, J. S., Villa, R. A., Nevin, A. I., & Harris, C. (2007). Accompanying DVD and Video for *Differentiated instruction: Collaborative planning and teaching for universally designed learning: A Multimedia Kit for Professional Development.* Thousand Oaks, CA: Corwin Press.

Torrence-Mikulecky, M., & Baber, A. (2005, December). *ECS Policy Brief: From highly qualified to highly competent paraprofessionals: how NCLB requirements can catalyze effective program and policy development—Guidelines from the ECS Paraprofessional expert panel.* Denver, CO: Education Commission of the States.

Villa, R., Thousand, J., & Nevin, A. (2008a). *A guide to co-teaching: Practical tips for facilitating student learning* (2nd ed.) Thousand Oaks, CA: Corwin Press.

Villa, R., Thousand, J., & Nevin, A. (2008b). *A guide to co-teaching multimedia kit.* Thousand Oaks, CA: Corwin Press.

Villa, R., Thousand, J., & Nevin, A. (2008c). *Co-teaching at-a-glance* [laminated reference guide]. Port Chester, NY: National Professional Resources, Inc.

Villa, R. A., Thousand, J. S., Nevin, A. I., & Harris, C. (2008). Accompanying DVD and Video for *A guide to co-teaching: Practical tips for facilitating student learning: A Multimedia Kit for Professional Development.* Thousand Oaks, CA: Corwin Press.

Webb-Johnson, G. C. (2002). Strategies for creating multicultural and pluralistic societies: A mind is a wonderful thing to develop. In J. S. Thousand, R. A. Villa, & A. I. Nevin. *Creativity and collaborative learning: The practical guide to empowering students, teachers, and families* (2nd ed., pp. 55–70). Baltimore: Paul H. Brookes Publishing Co.

Wenger, K., Lubbes, T., Lazo, M., Azcarraga, I., Sharp, S., & Ernst-Slavit, G. (2004). Hidden teachers, invisible students: Lessons learned from exemplary bilingual paraprofessionals in secondary schools. *Teacher Education Quarterly, 31*(2), 89–111.

Werts, M., Zigmond, N., & Leeper, D. (2001). Paraprofessional proximity and academic engagement: Students with disabilities in primary aged classrooms. *Education and Training in Mental Retardation and Developmental Disabilities, 36*(4), 424–440.

Yarger, C. (1996). Notetaking programs: Starting out right! *Perspectives in Education and Deafness, 15*(1), 6–8, 20–21.

Young, B. (1997). An examination of paraprofessional involvement in supporting inclusion of students with autism. *Focus on Autism and Other Developmental Disabilities, 12*(1), 31–38, 48.

Index

CORWIN PRESS

The Corwin Press logo—a raven striding across an open book—represents the union of courage and learning. Corwin Press is committed to improving education for all learners by publishing books and other professional development resources for those serving the field of PreK–12 education. By providing practical, hands-on materials, Corwin Press continues to carry out the promise of its motto: **"Helping Educators Do Their Work Better."**

The worldwide mission of The Council for Exceptional Children is to improve educational outcomes for individuals with exceptionalities.

CEC, a non-profit association, accomplishes its mission, which is carried out in support of special education professionals and others working on behalf of individuals with exceptionalities, by advocating for appropriate governmental policies, by setting professional standards, by providing continuing professional development, by advocating for newly and historically underserved individuals with exceptionalities, and by helping professionals achieve the conditions and resources necessary for effective professional practice.